UNICORN COLORING BOOK
For Adult & Teens
- RUSS FOCUS -

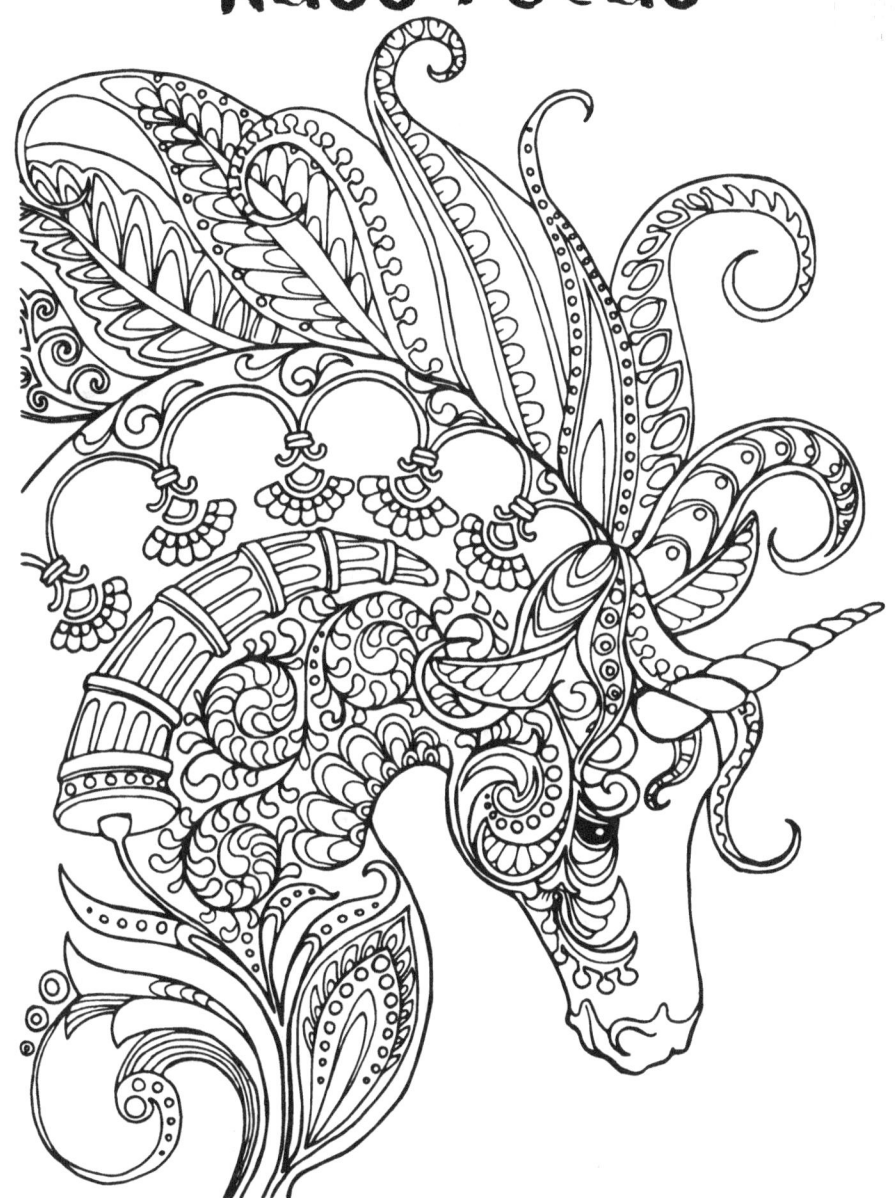

ISBN-13: 978-1720539902   ISBN-10: 1720539901

PUBLISHED BY RUSS FOCUS COPYRIGHT © 2018 ALL RIGHTS RESERVED

NO PART OF THIS PUBLICATION MAY BE REPRODUCED IN ANY

FORM OR BY ANY MEANS WITHOUT WRITTEN PERMISSION OF THE PUBLISHER.

WE ARE NOT RESPONSIBLE FOR UNSOLICITES MATERIAL PUBLISHED IN USA

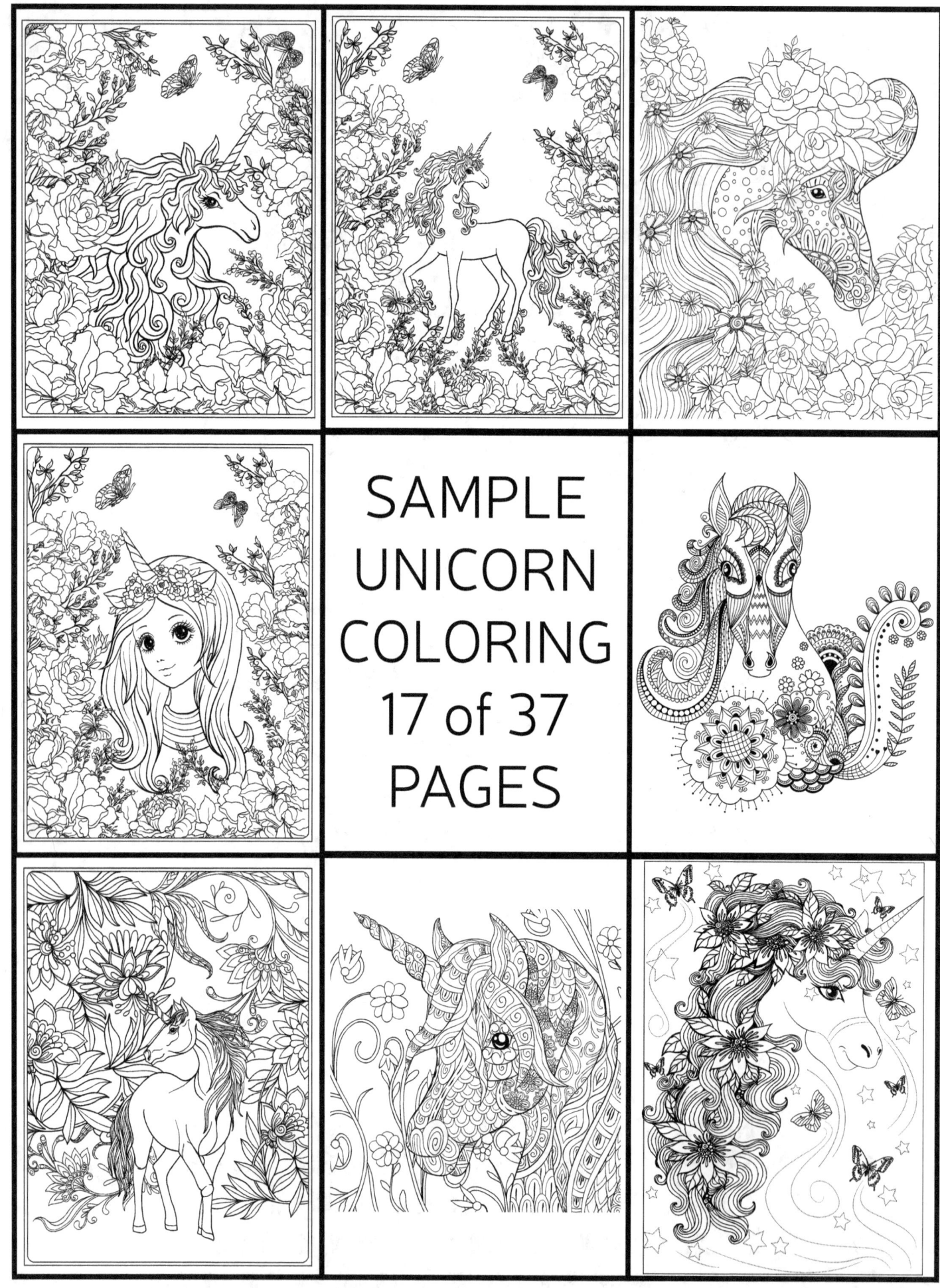

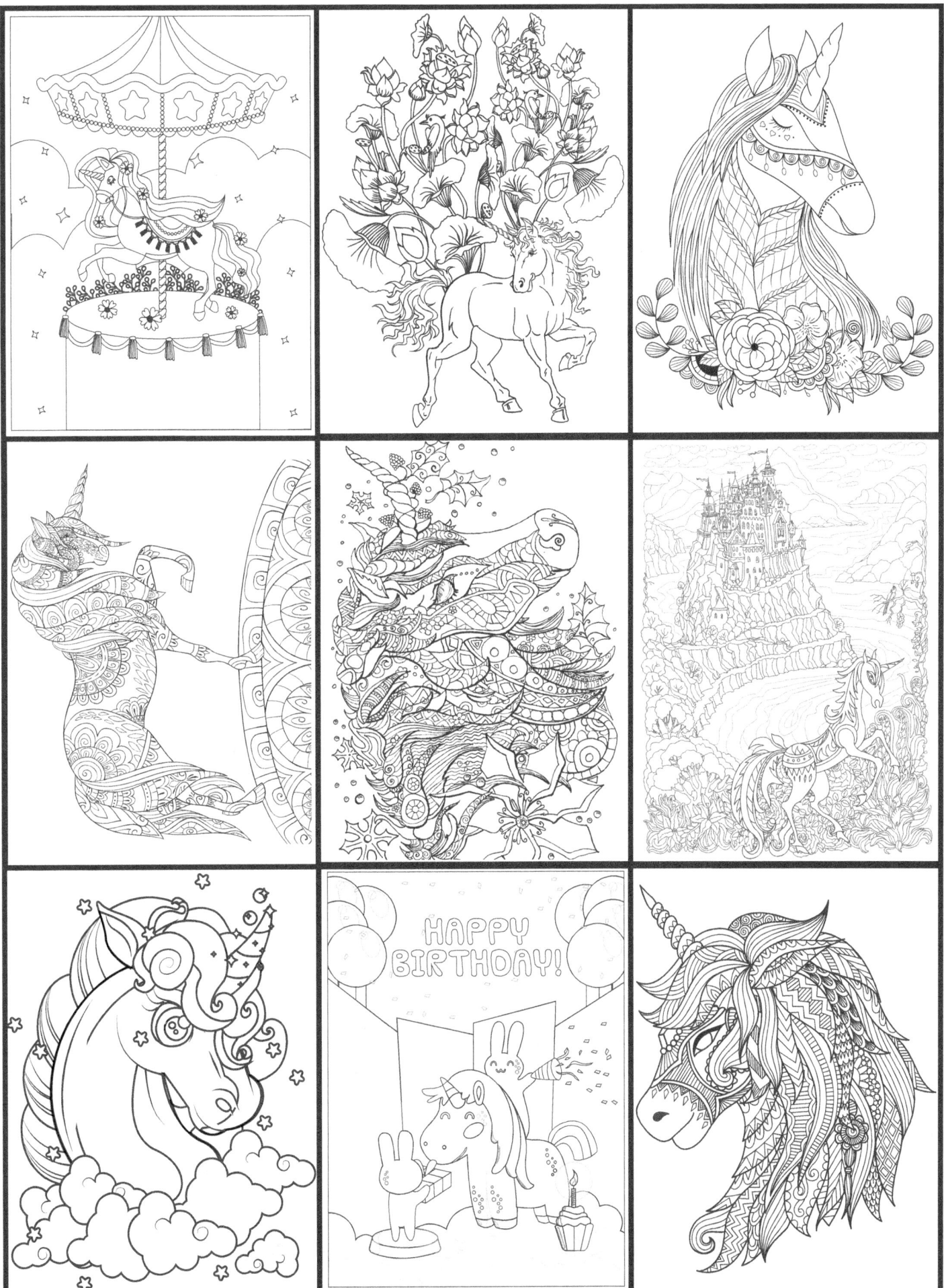

www.russfocus.com

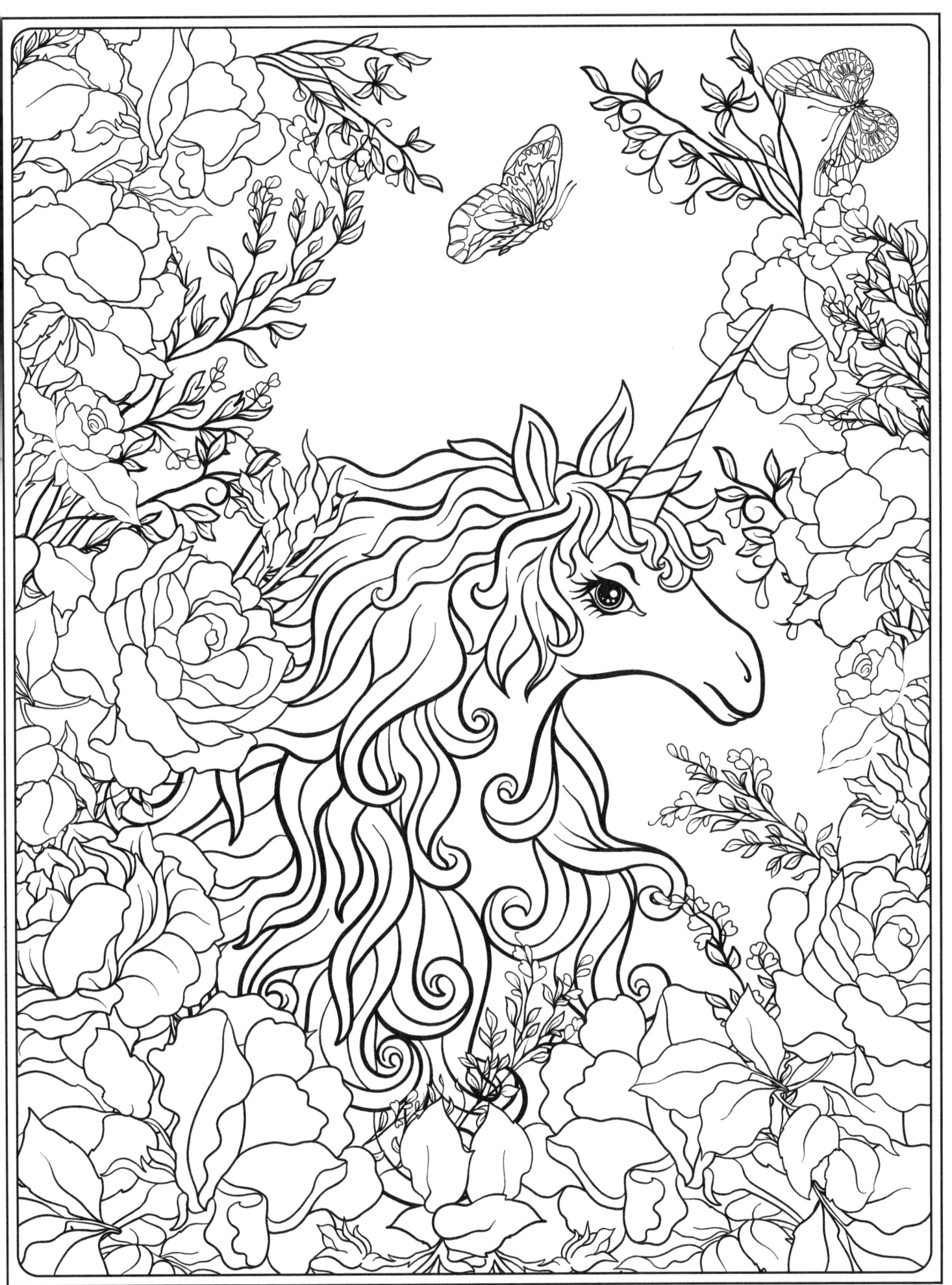

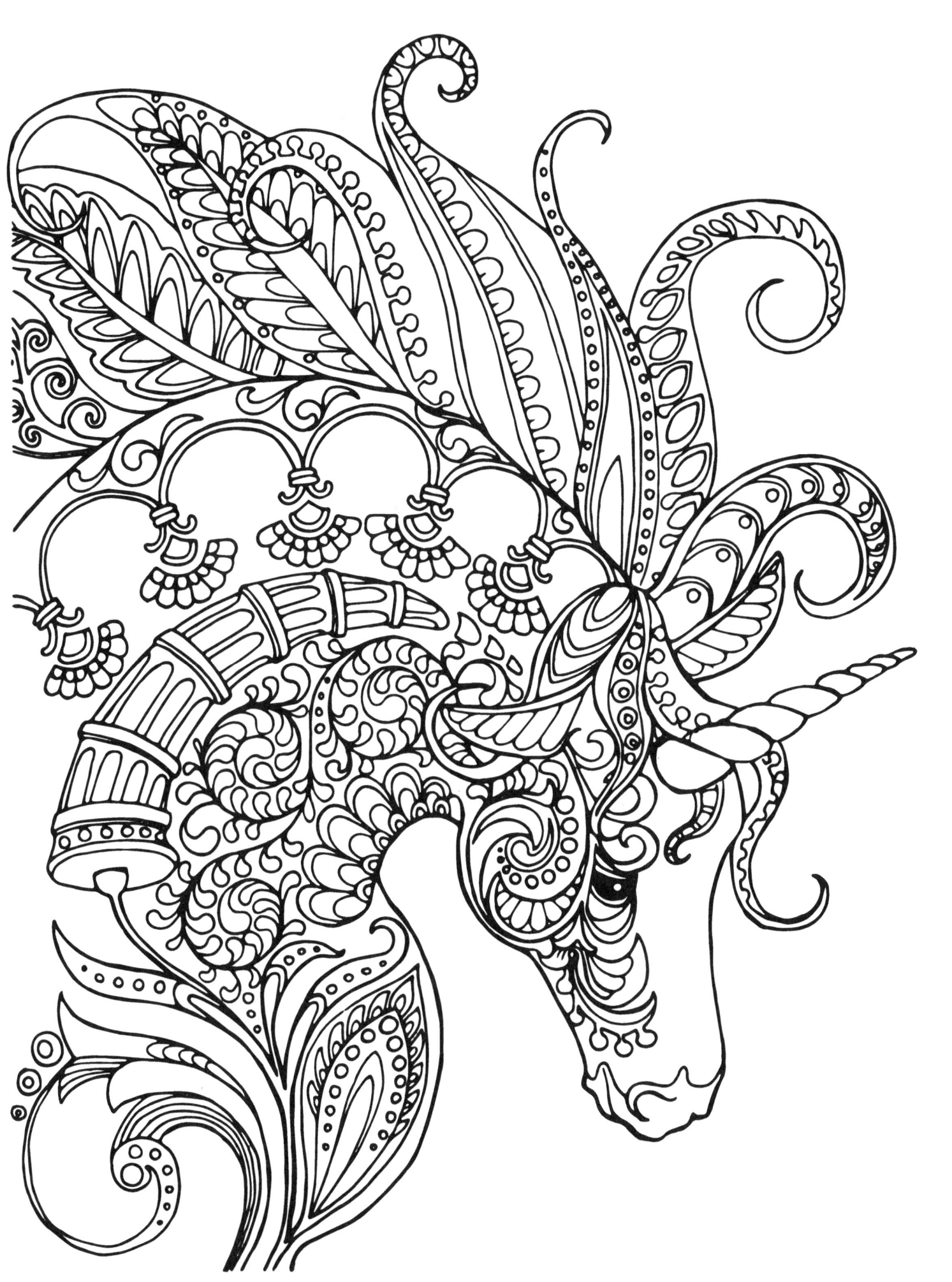

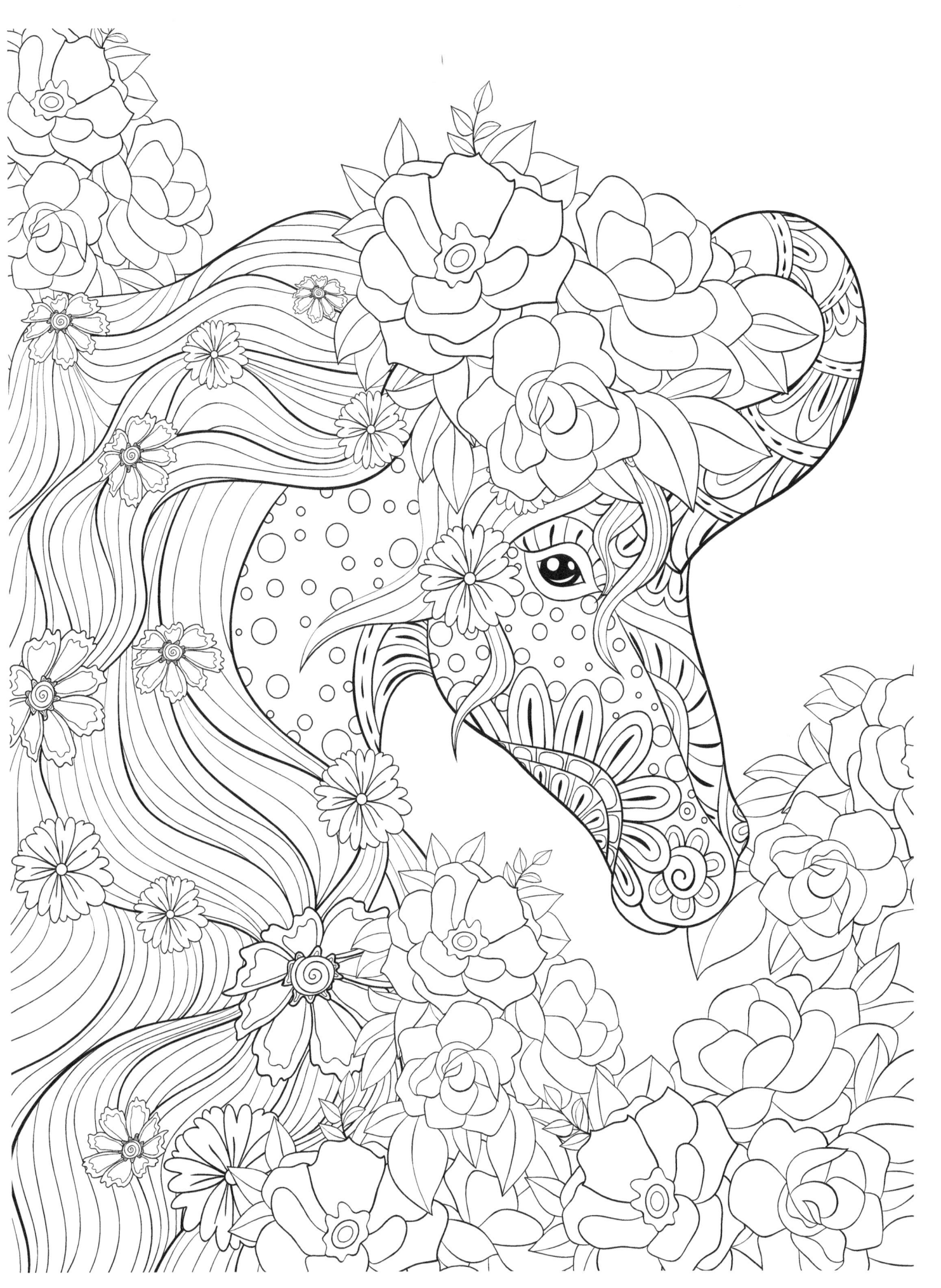

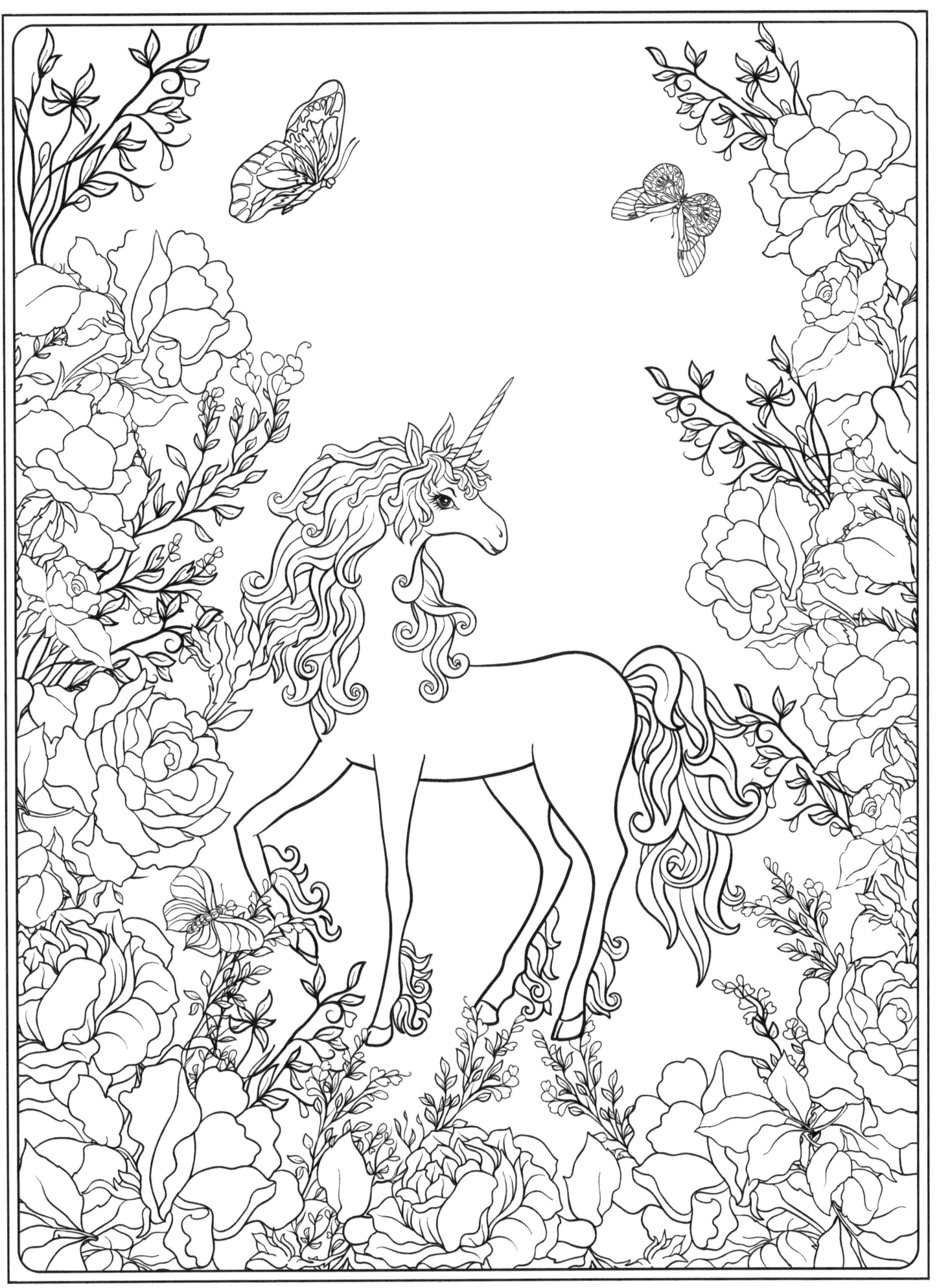

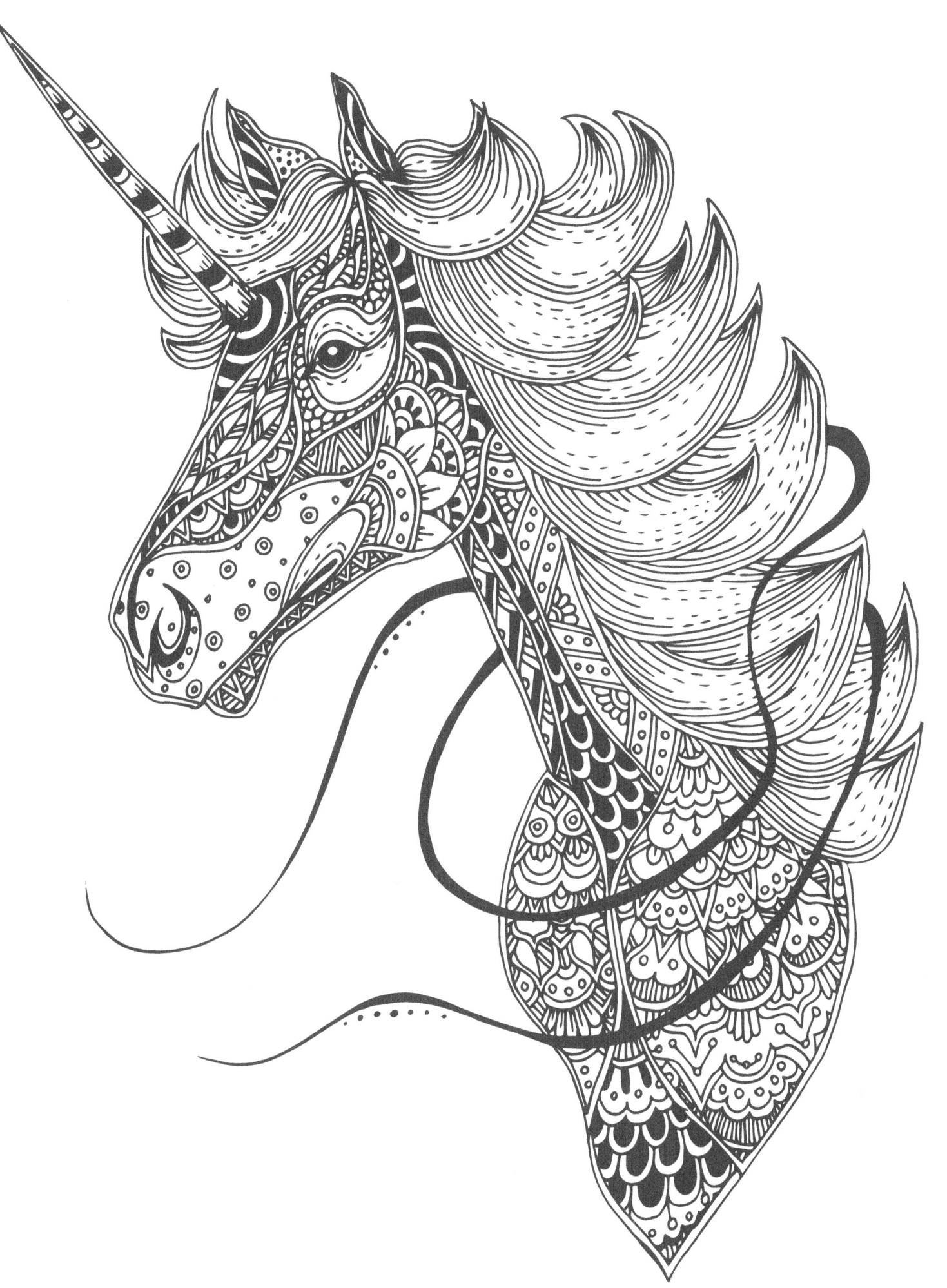

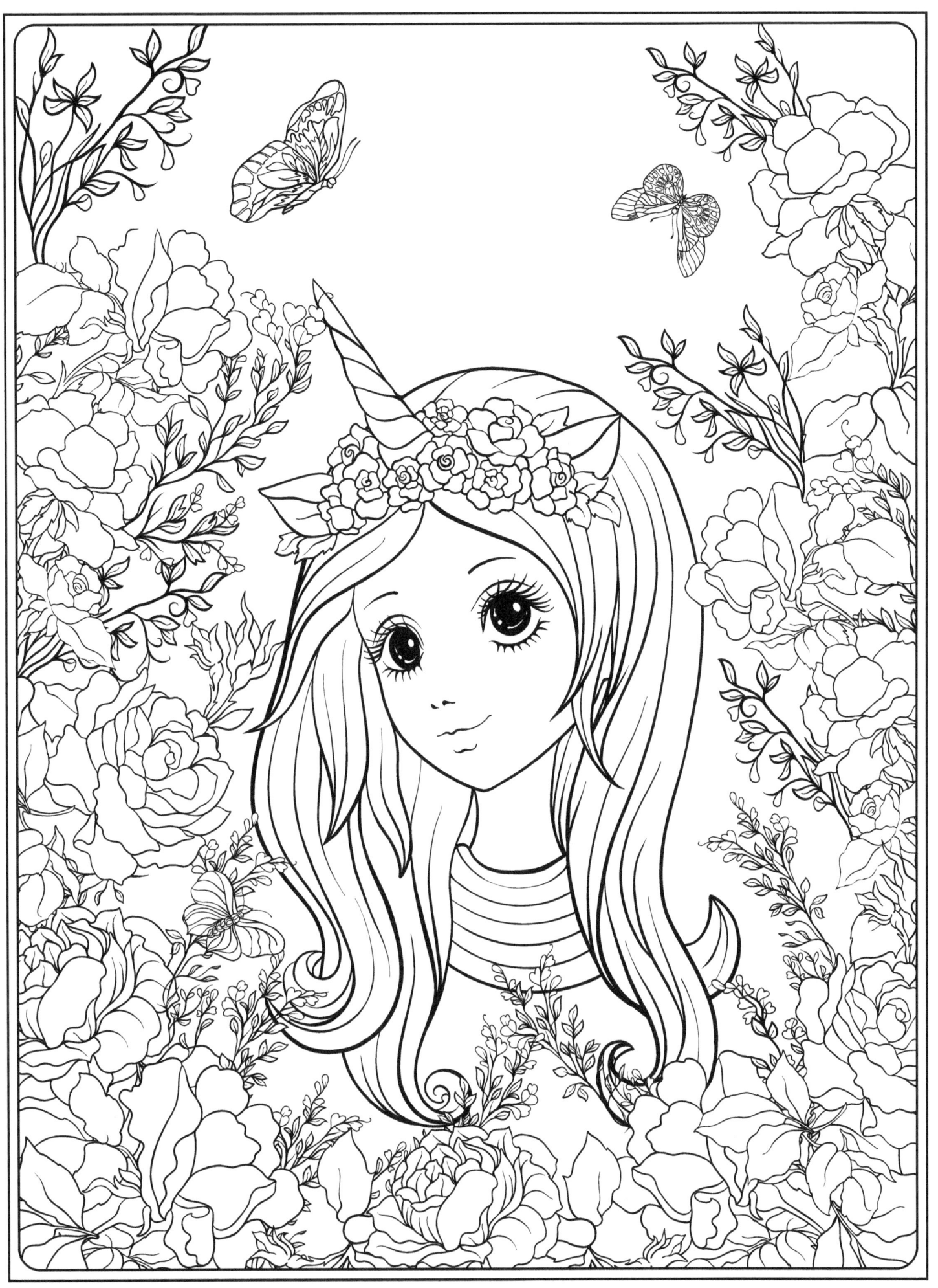

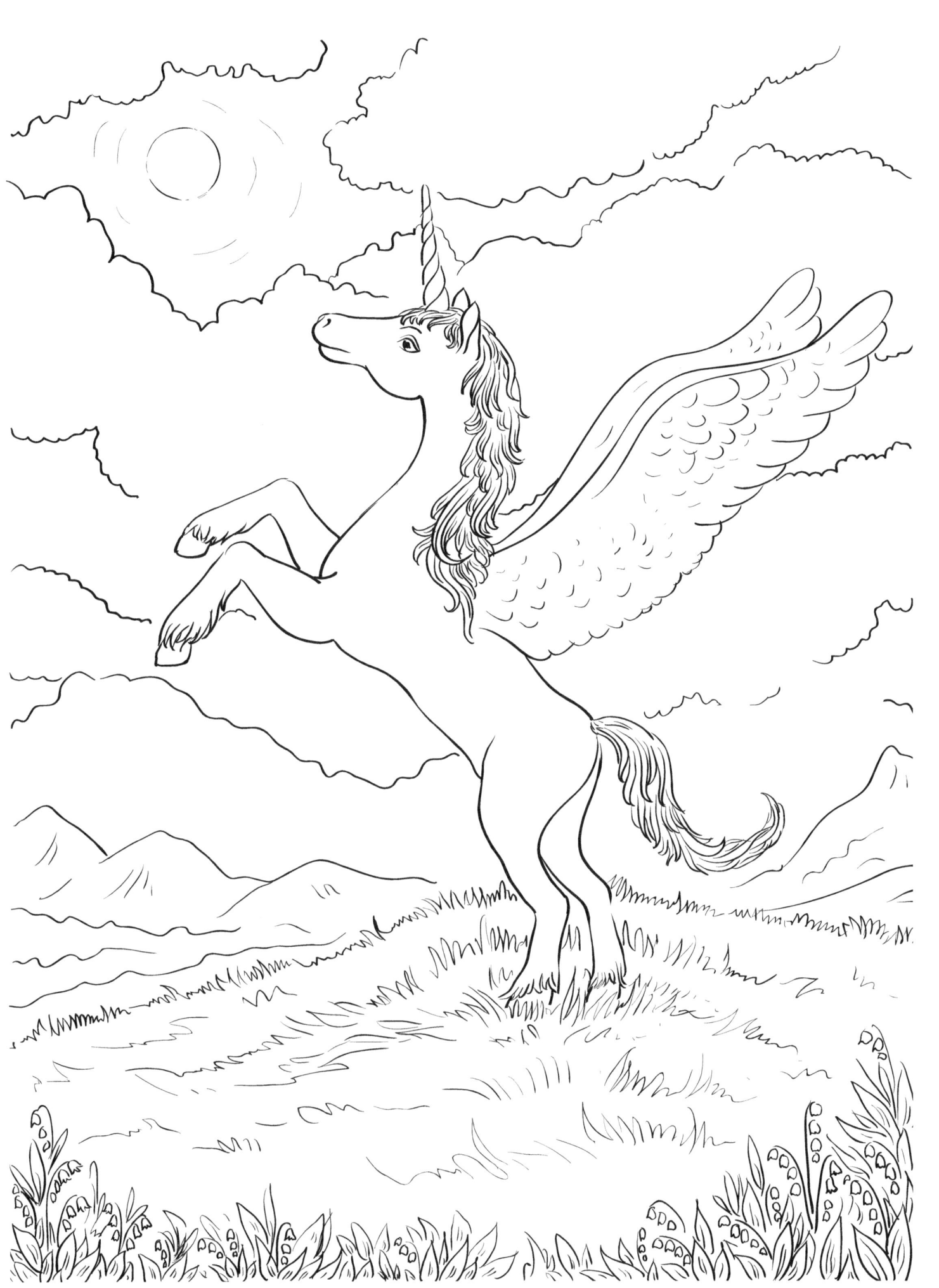

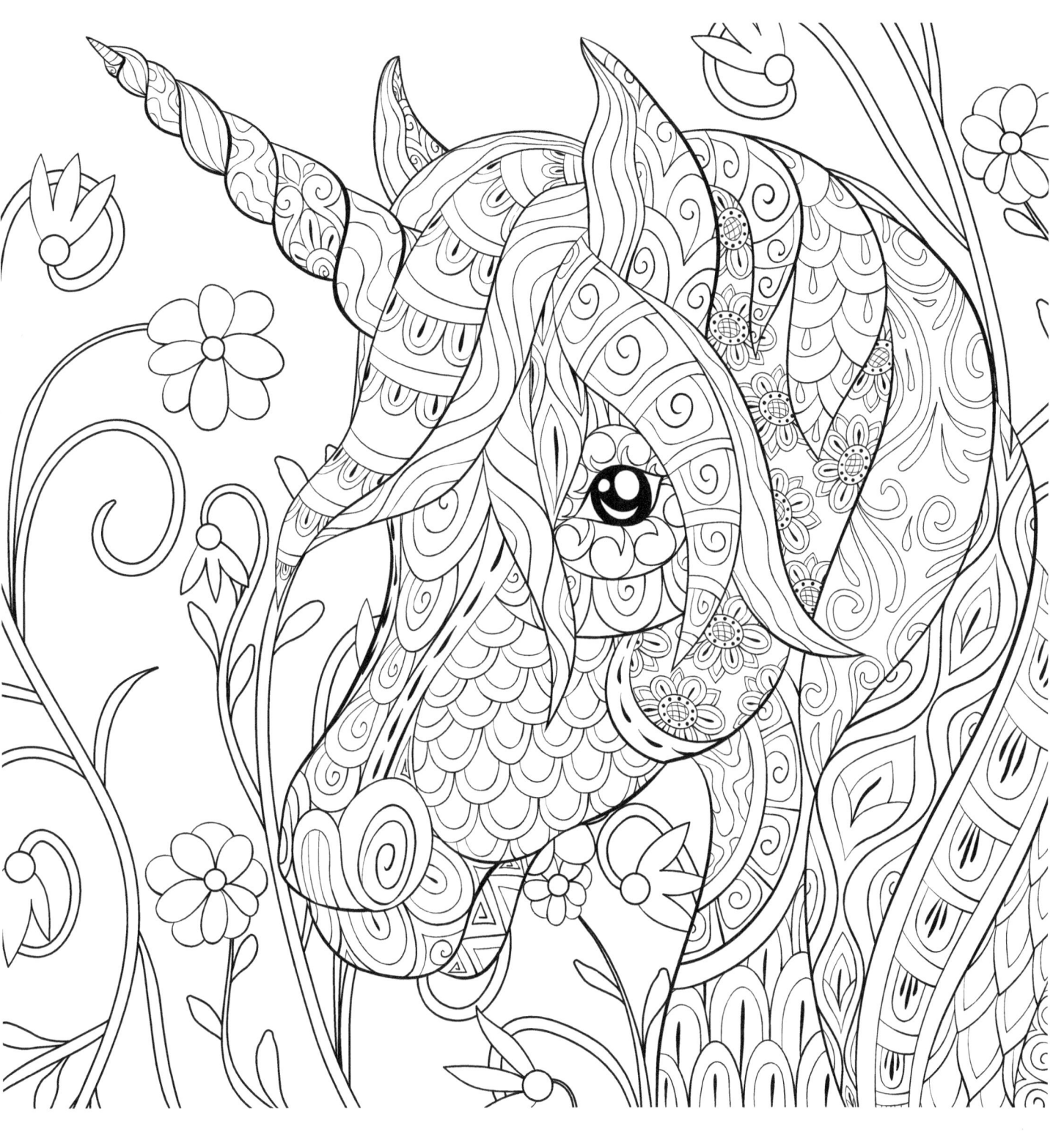

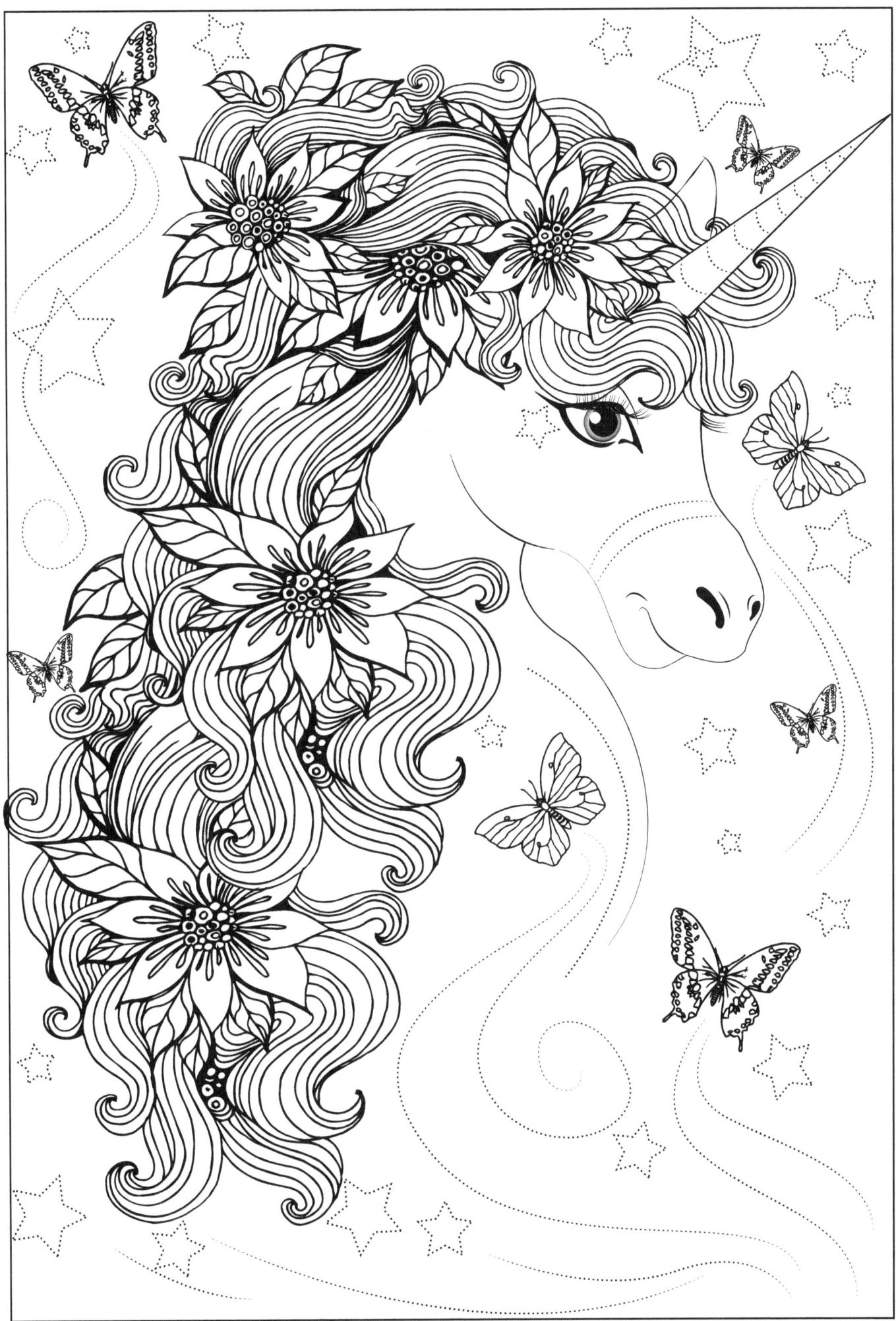

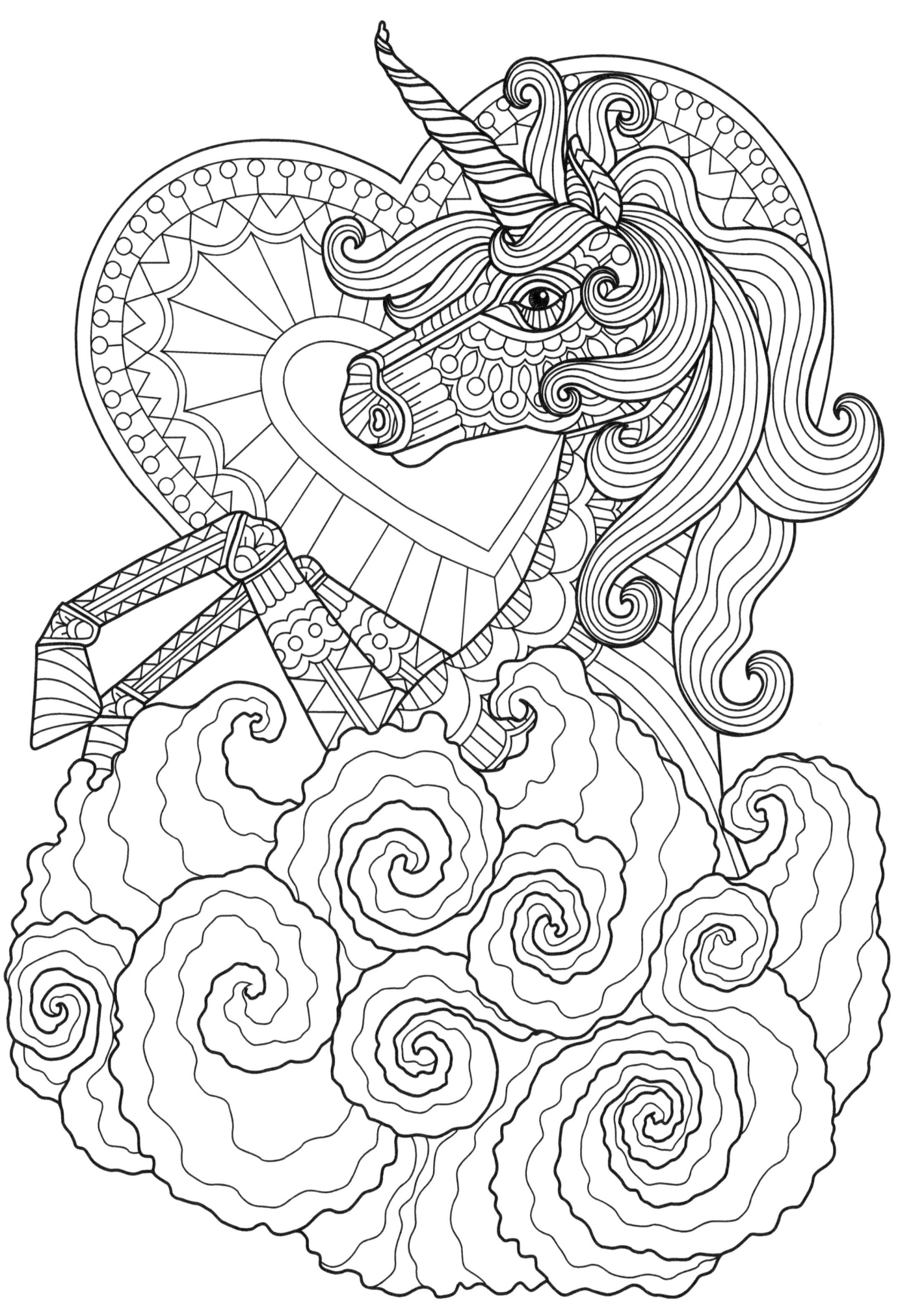

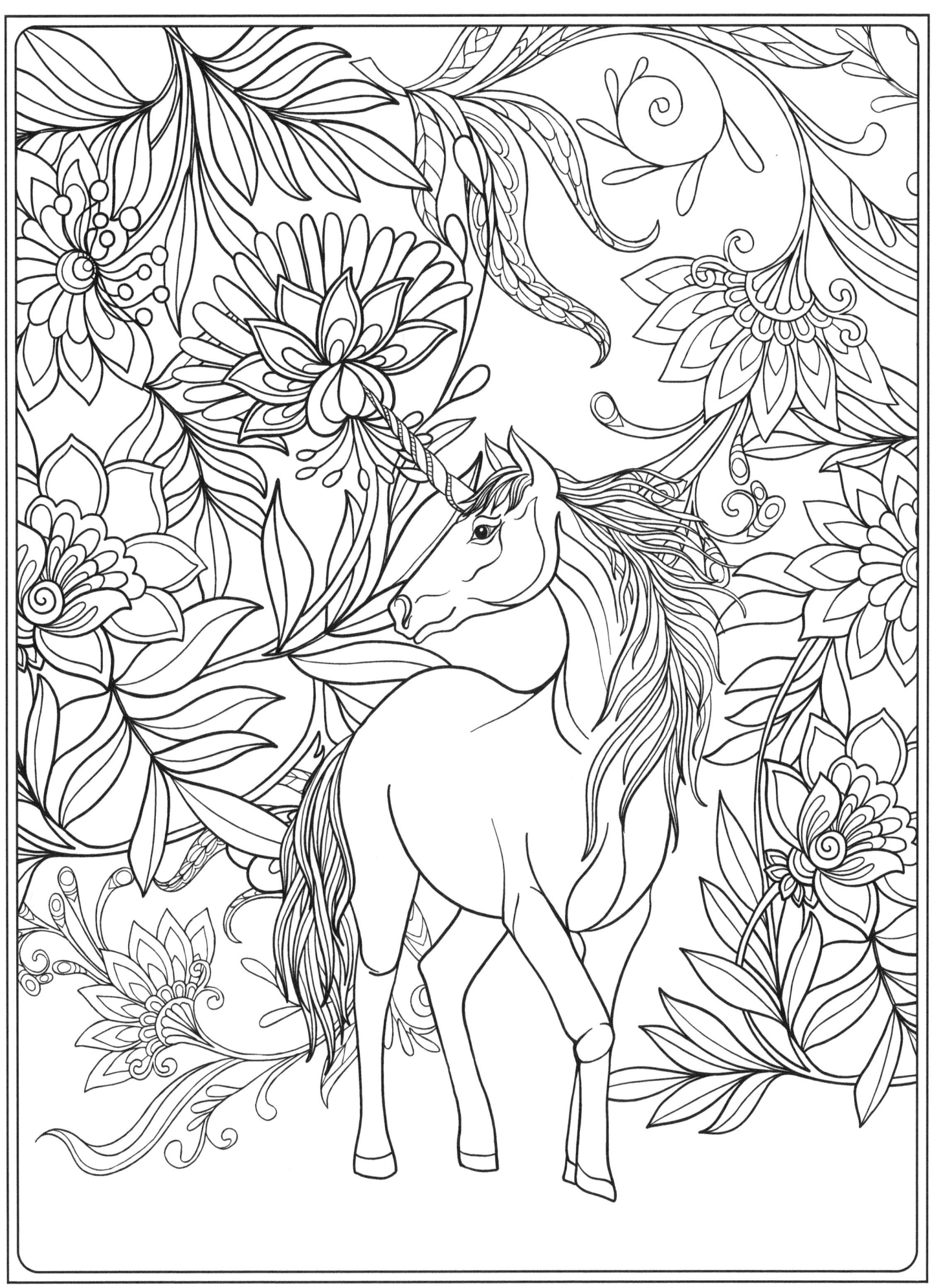

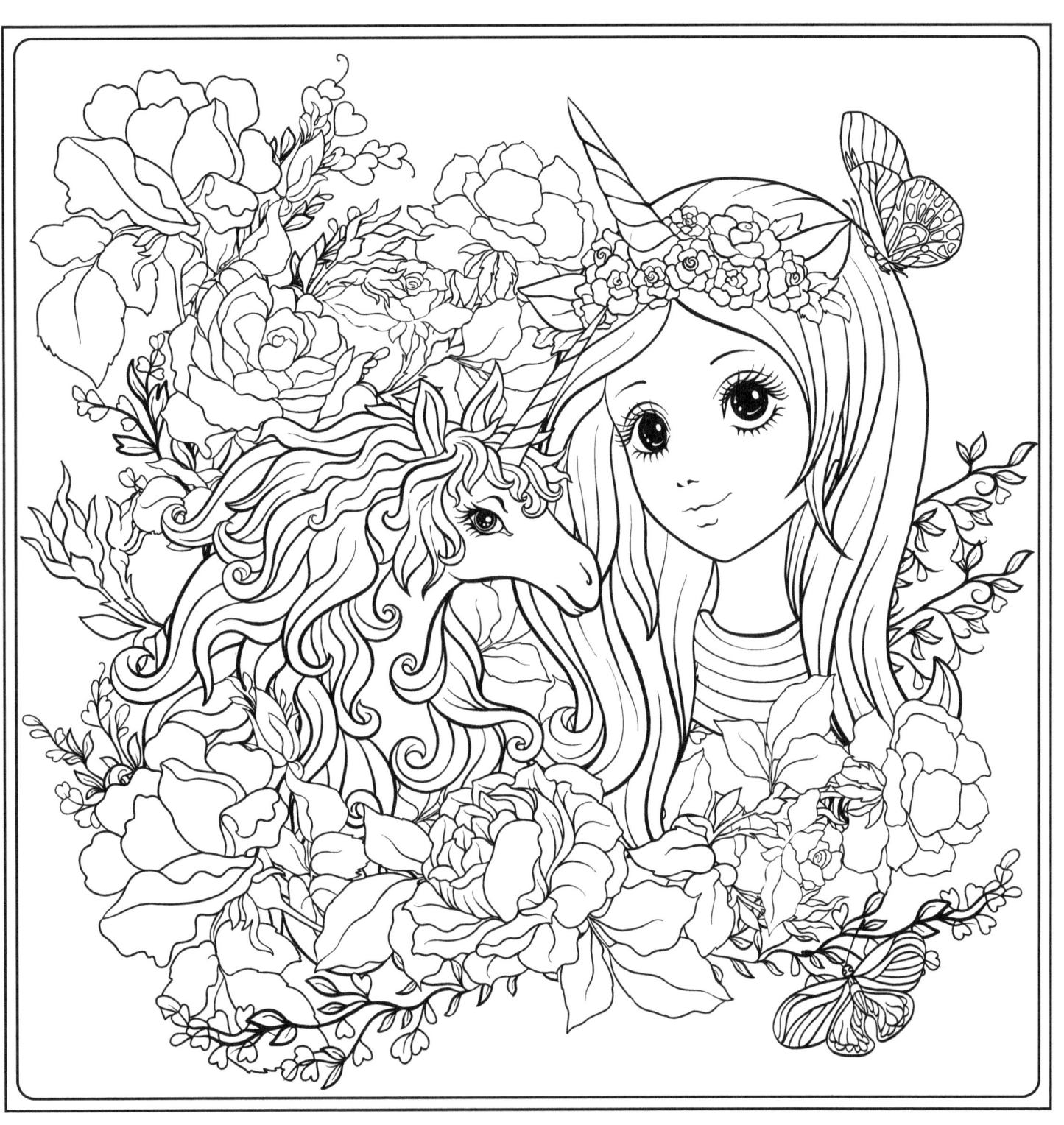

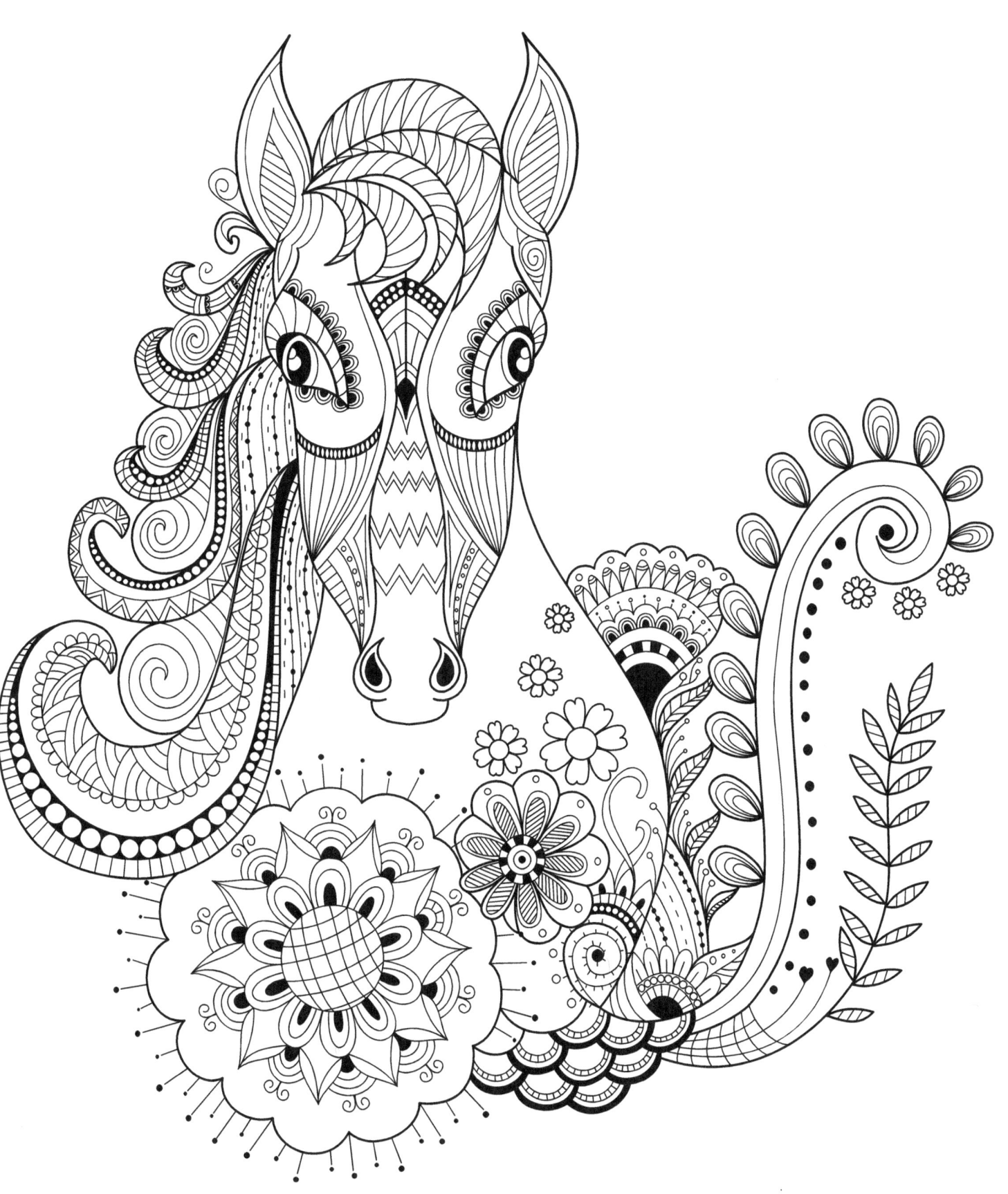

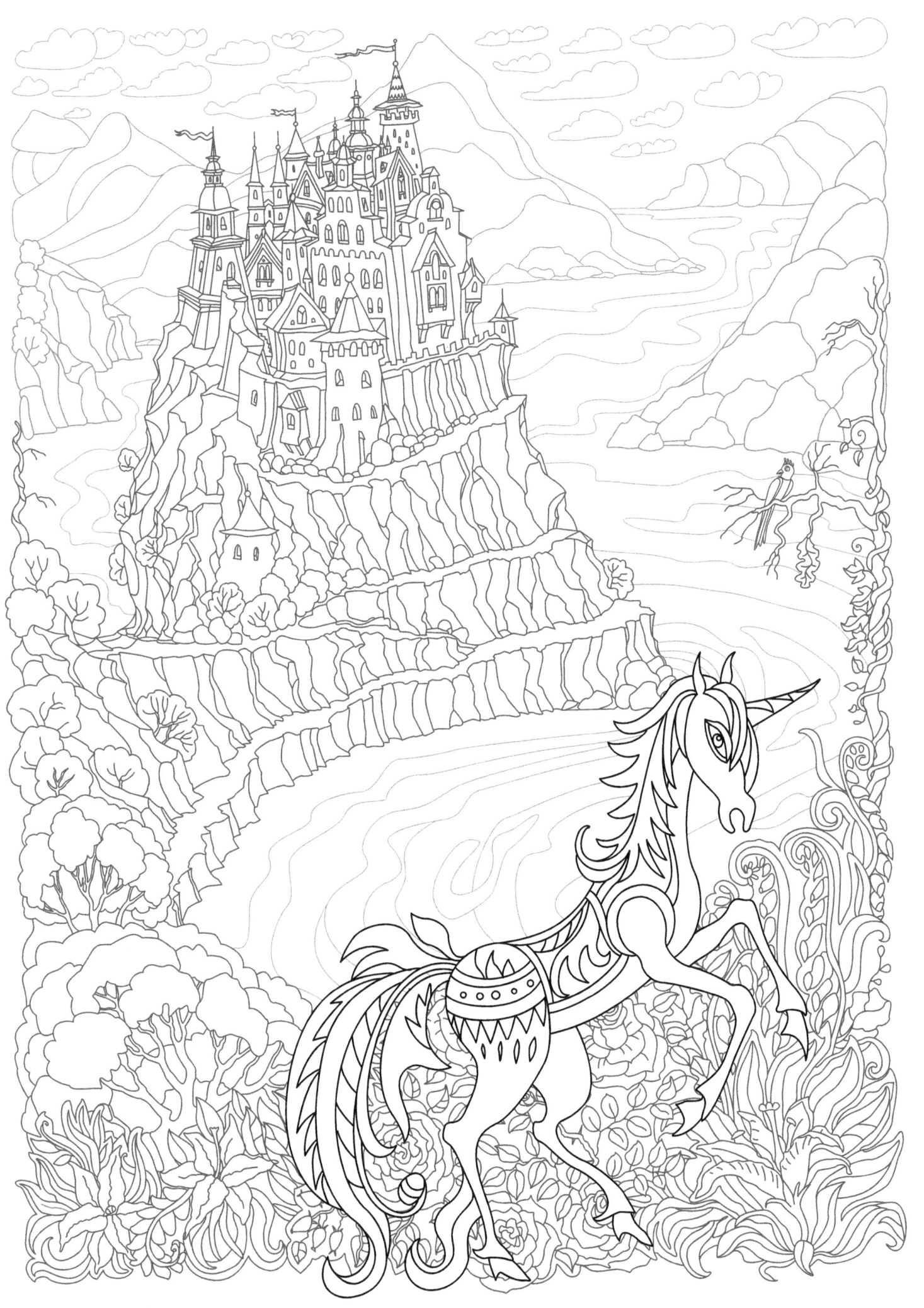

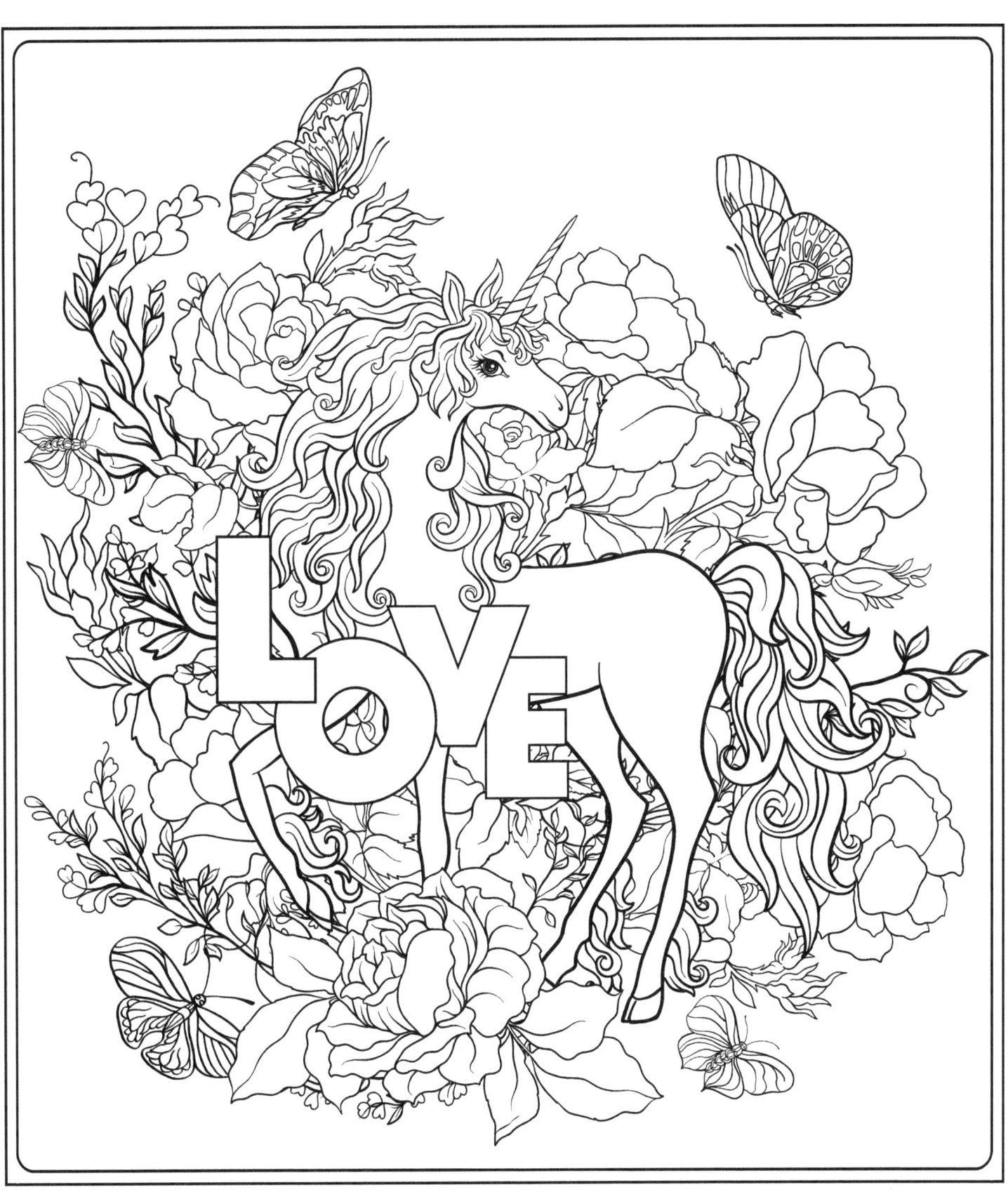

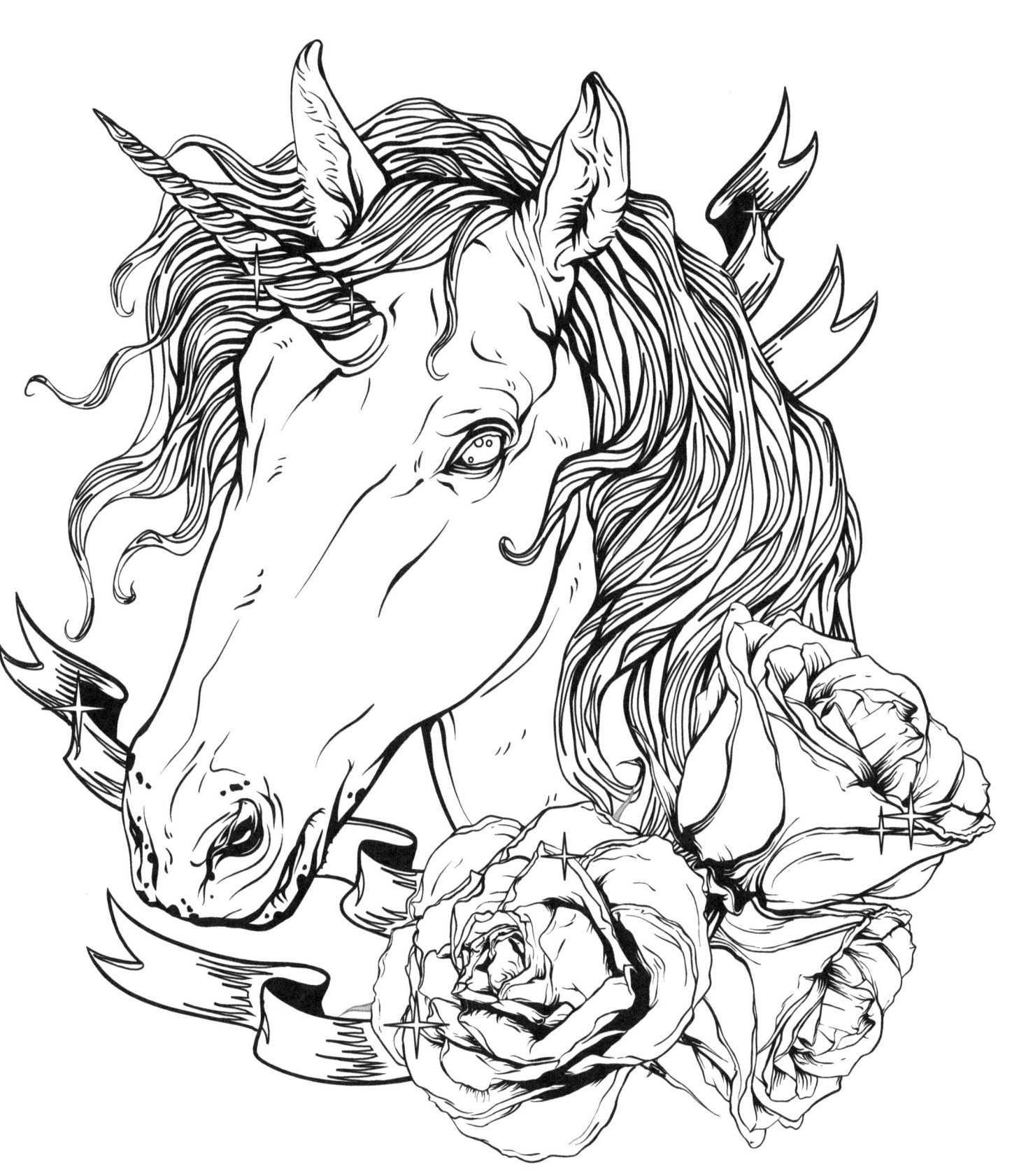

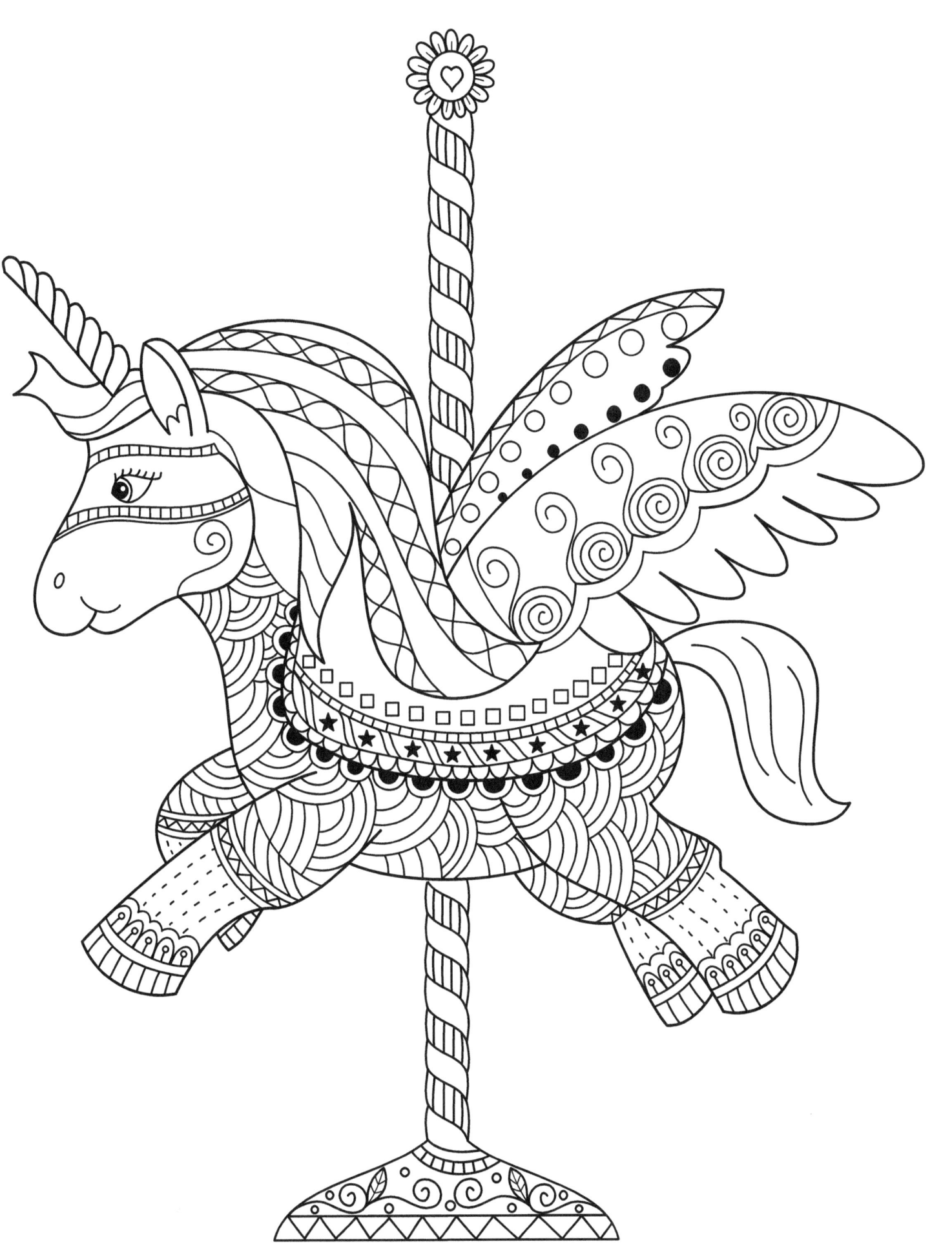

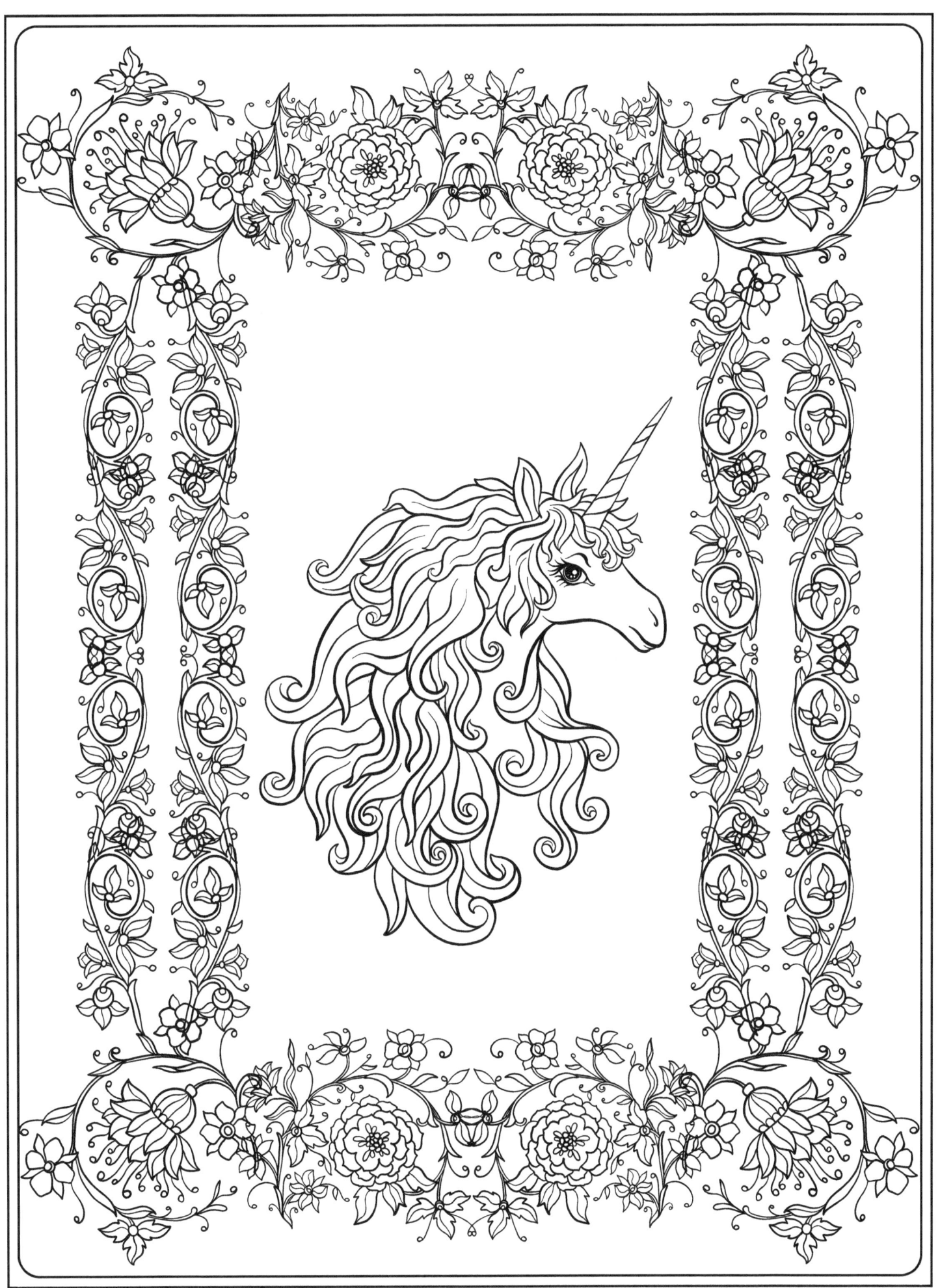

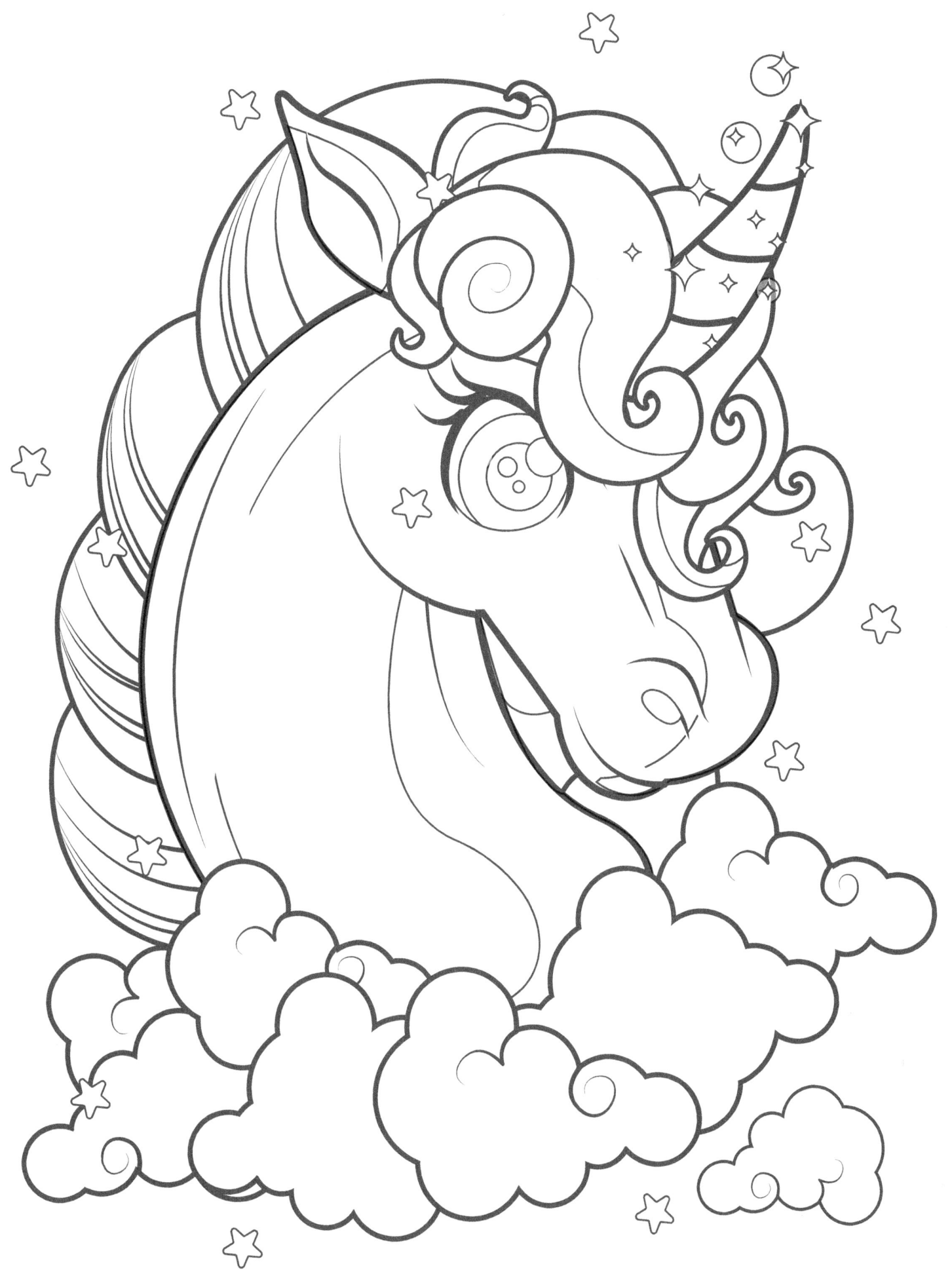

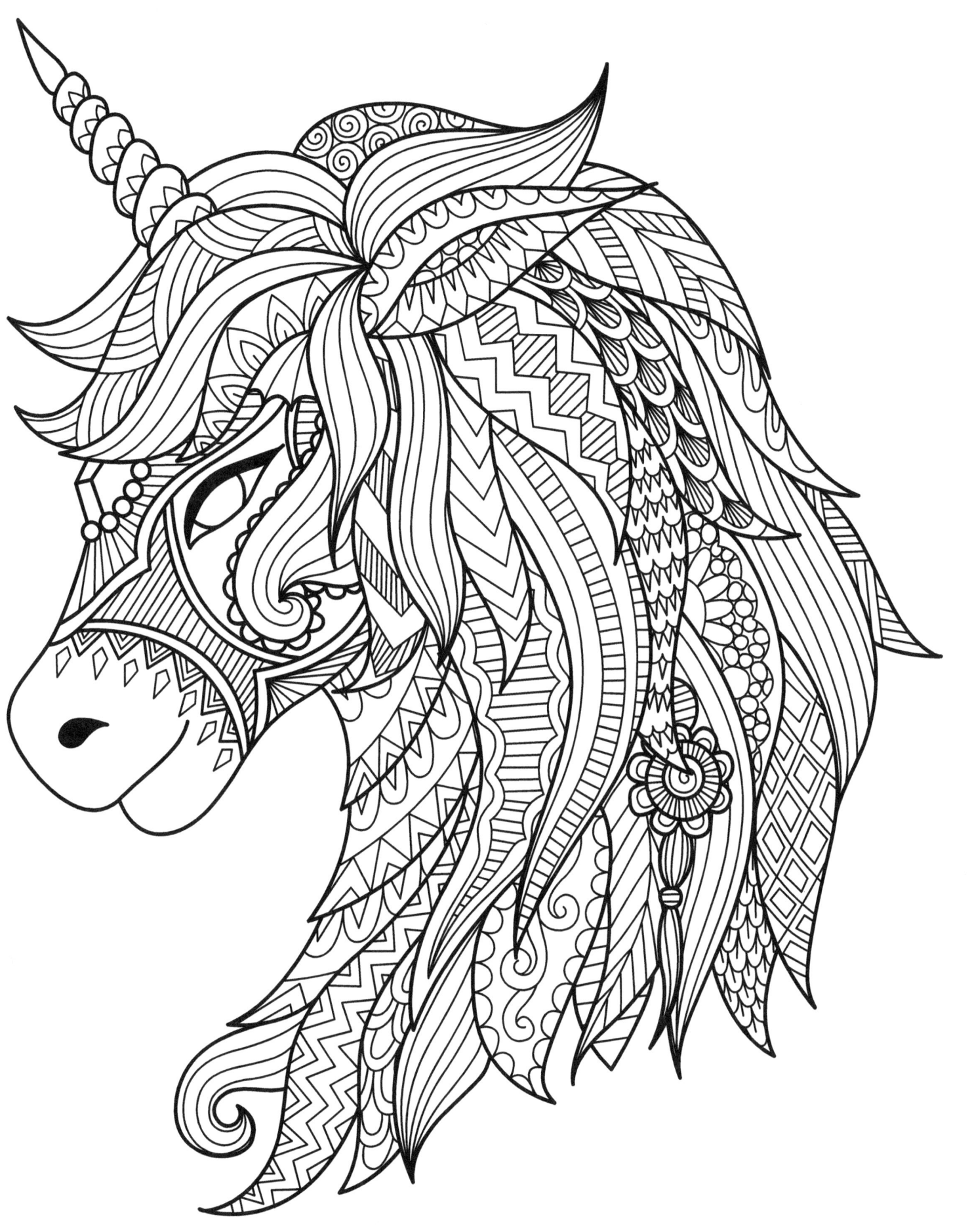

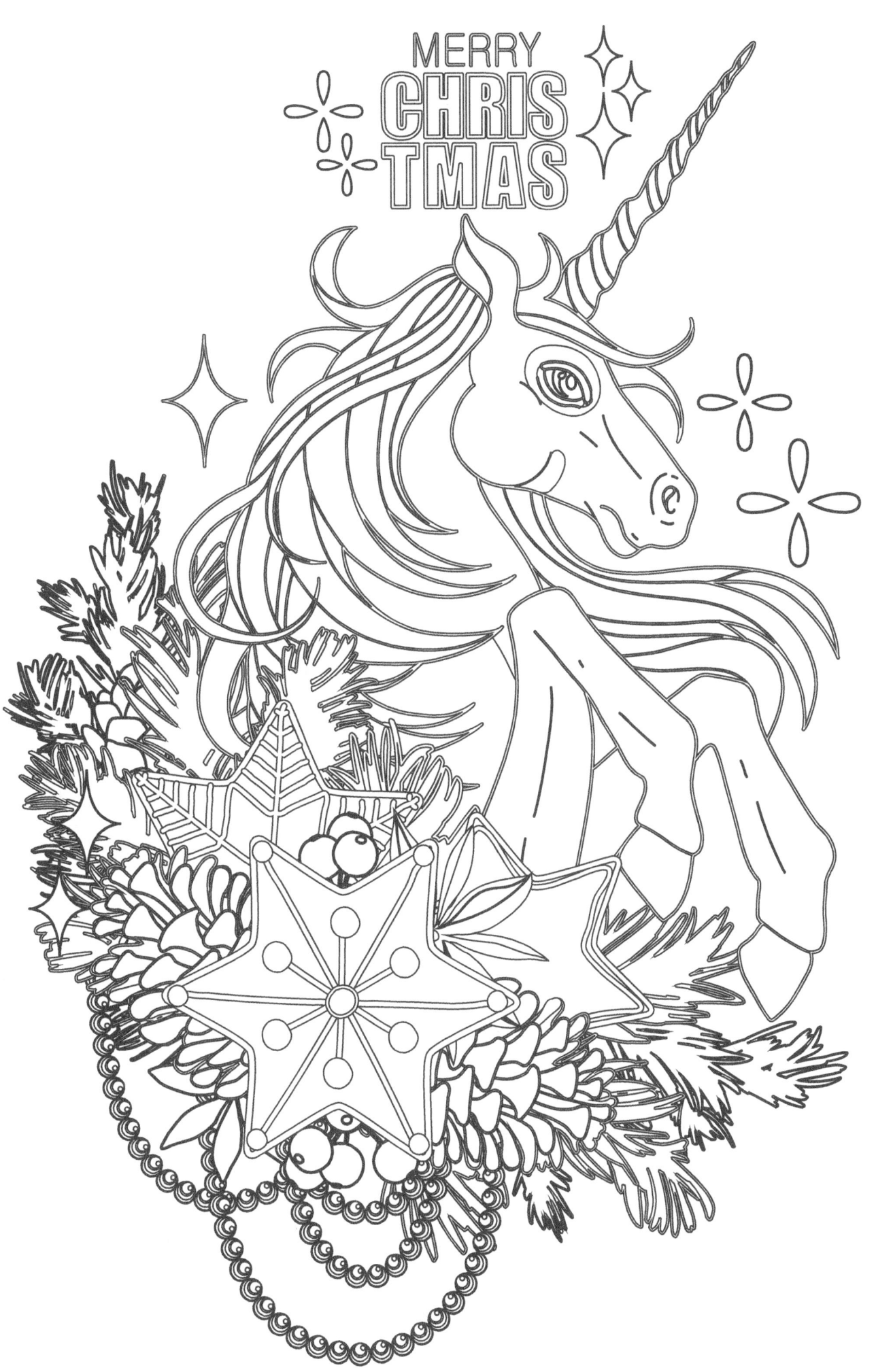

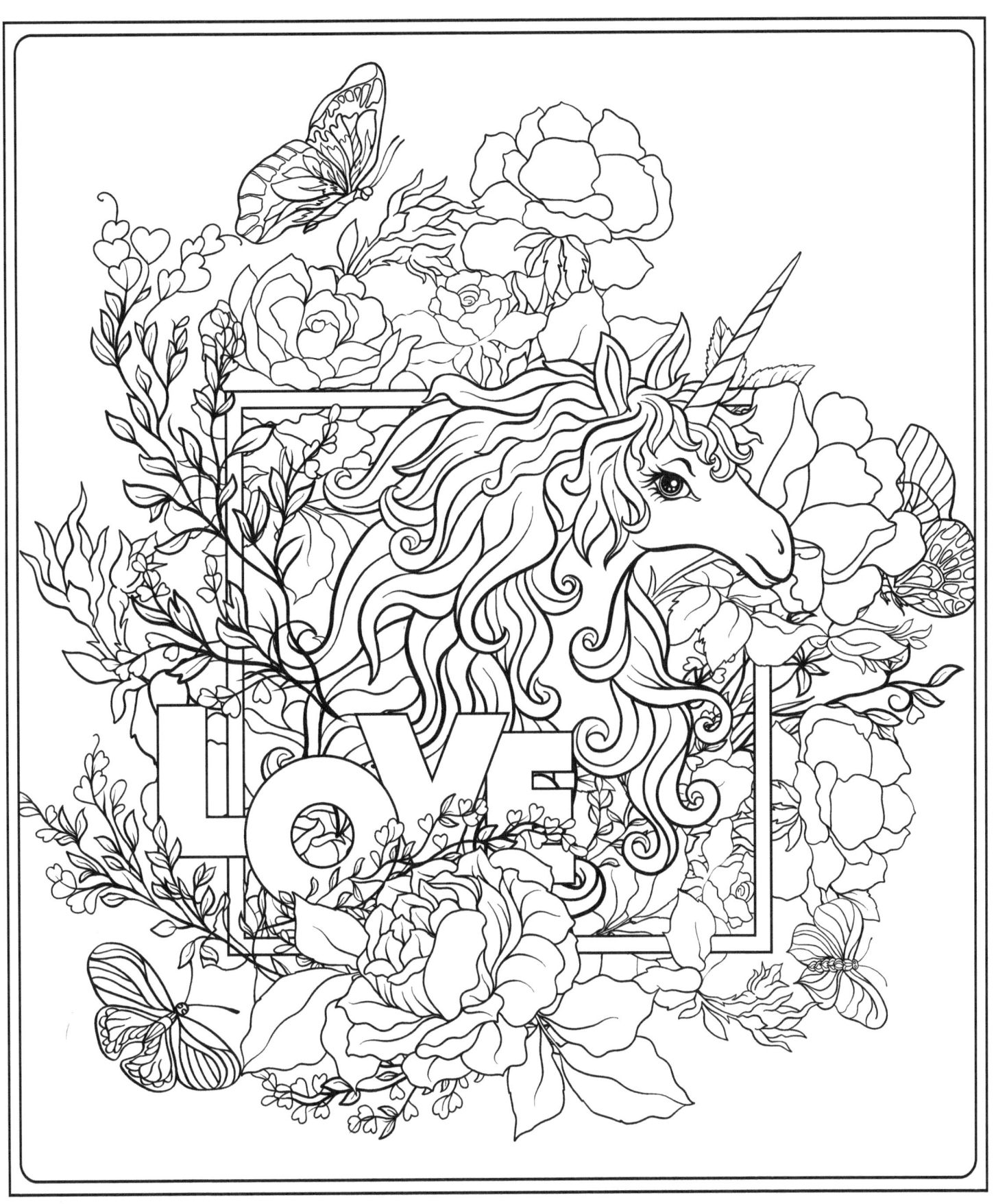

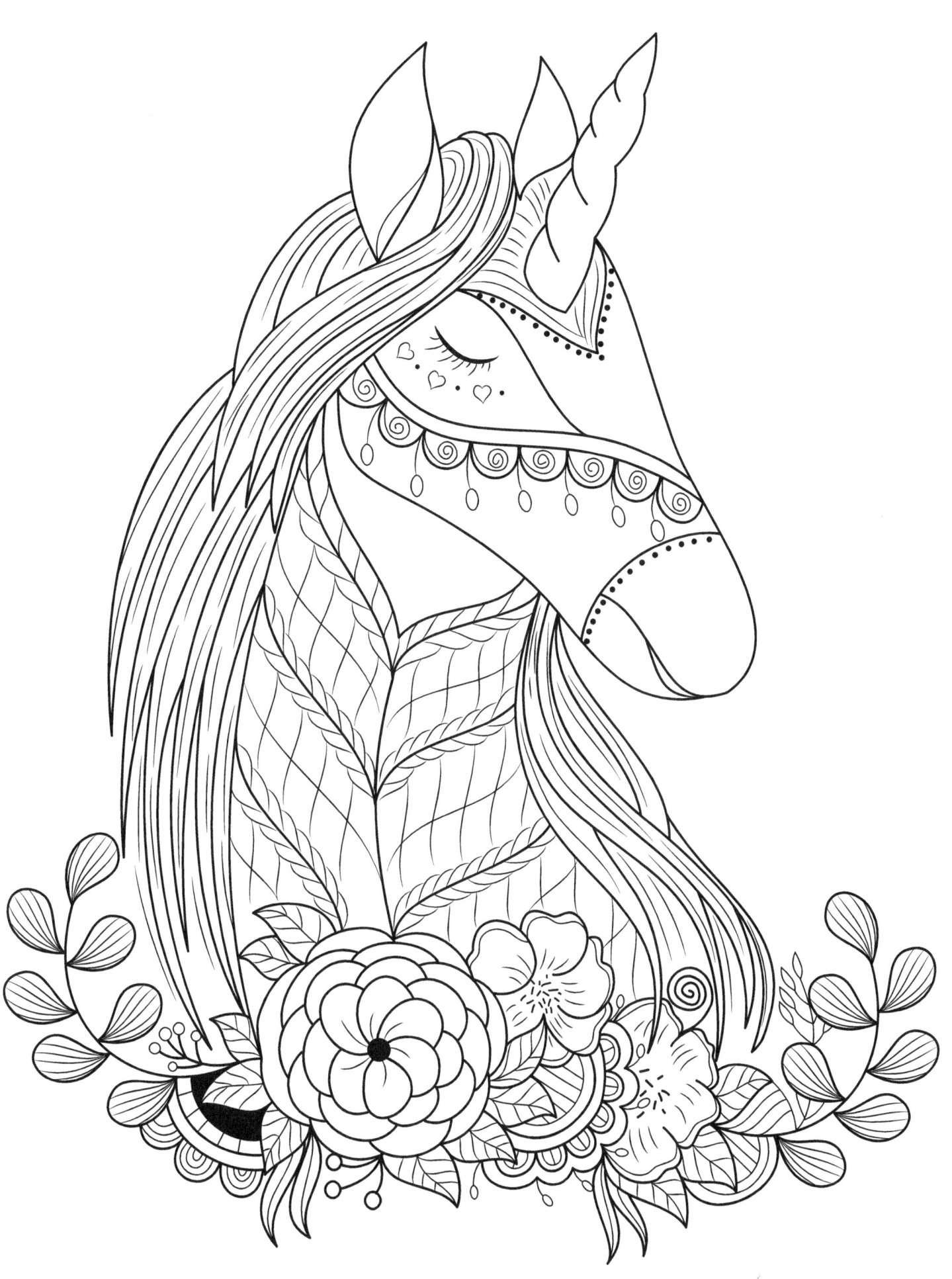

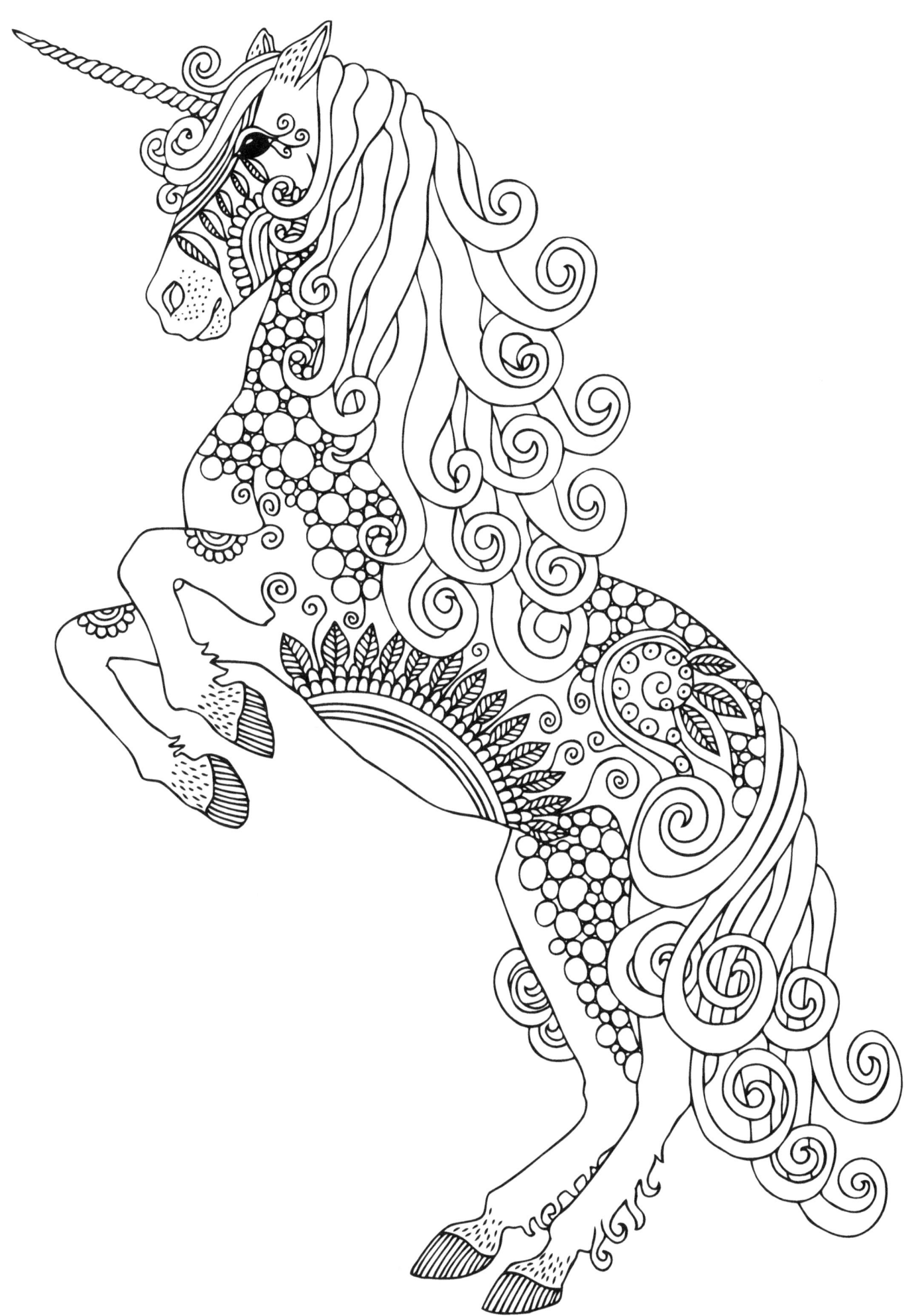

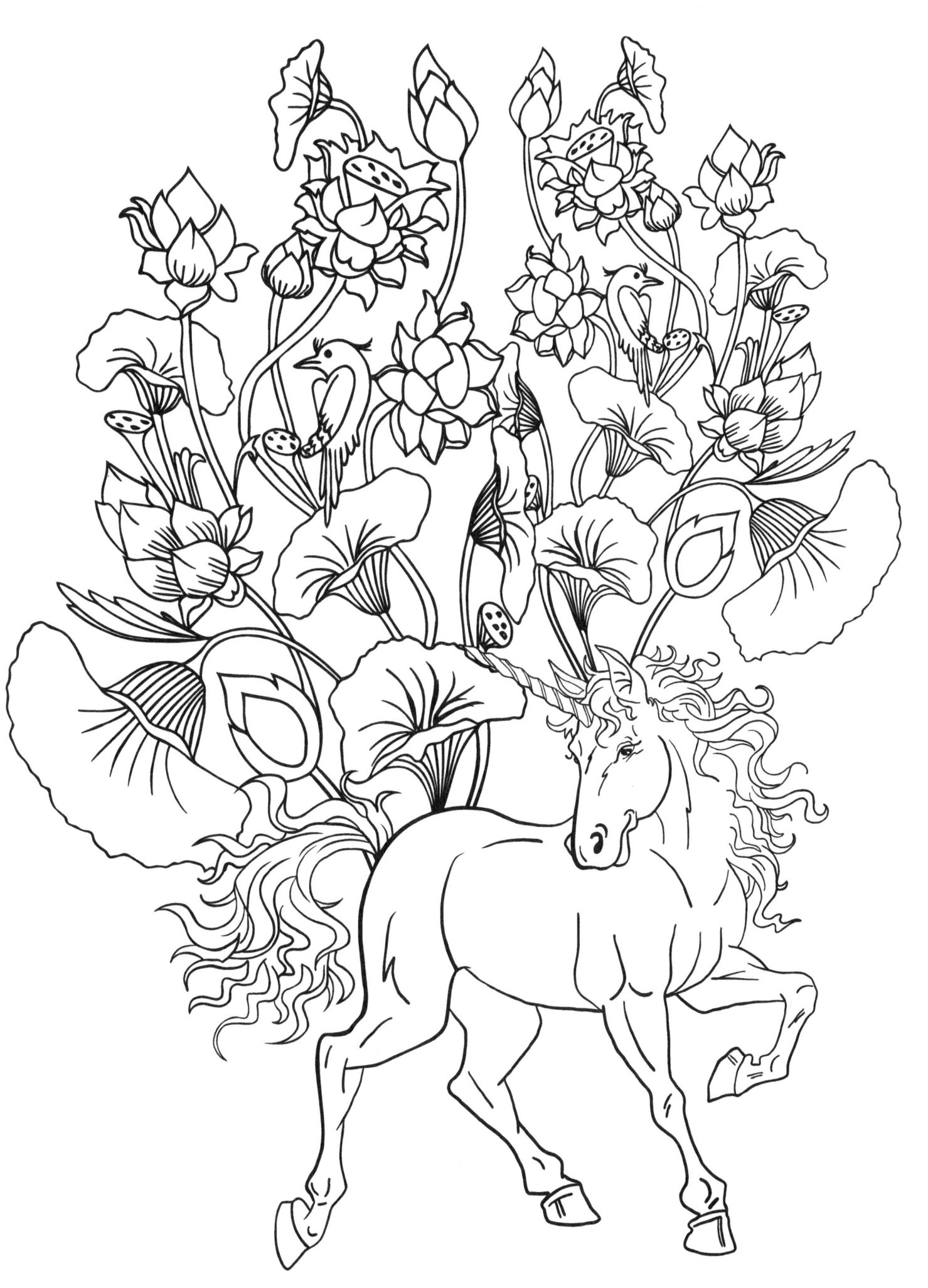

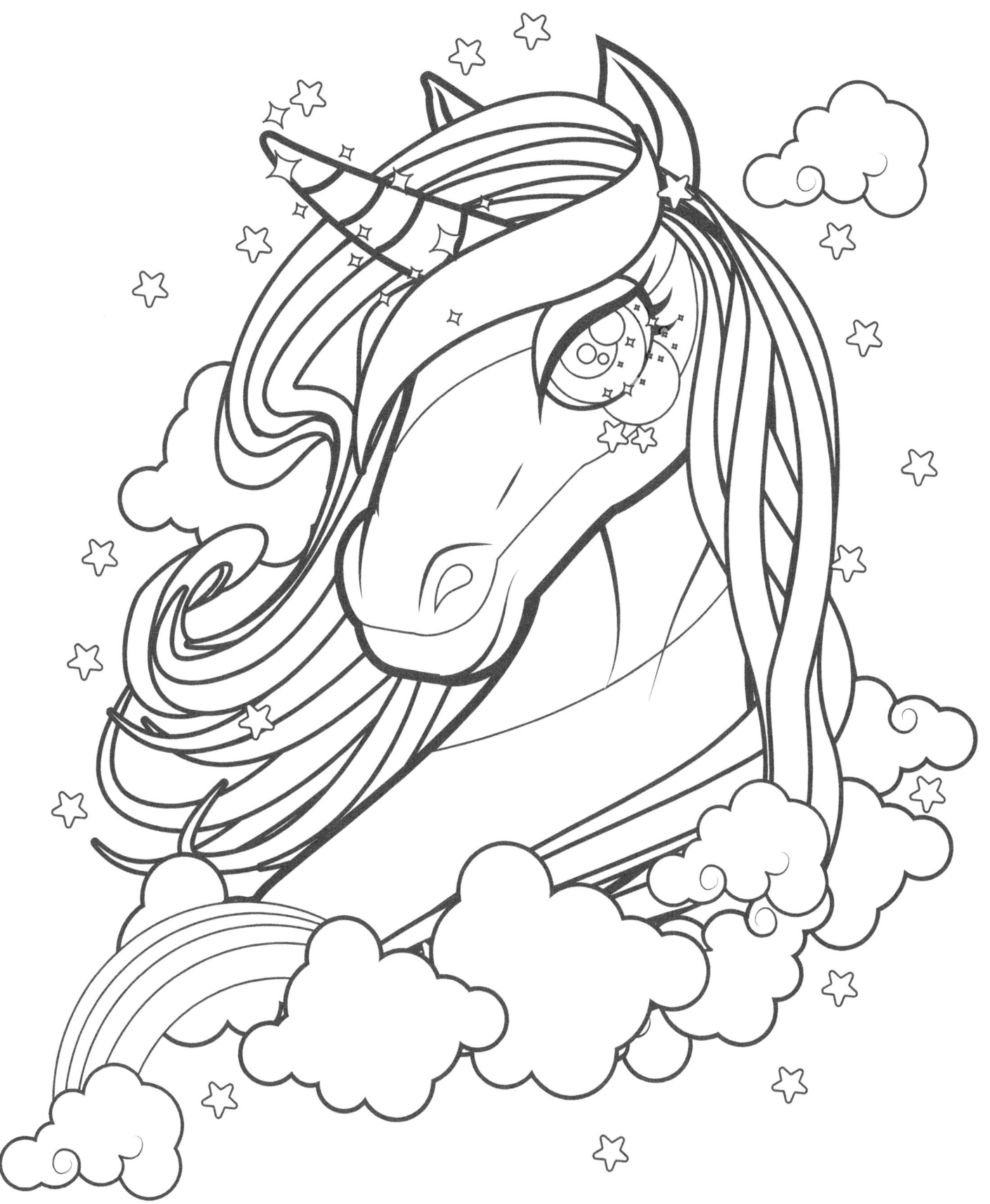

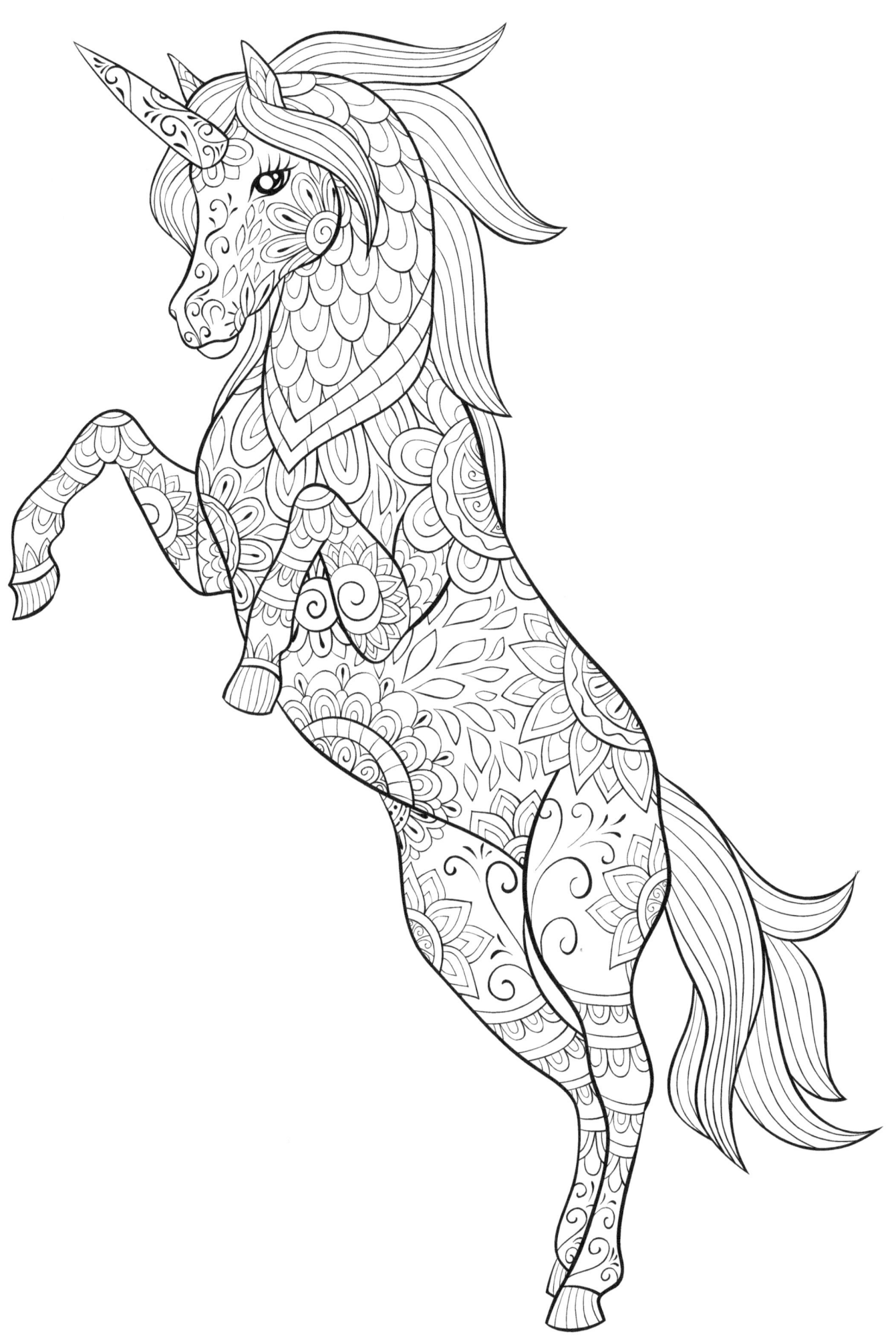

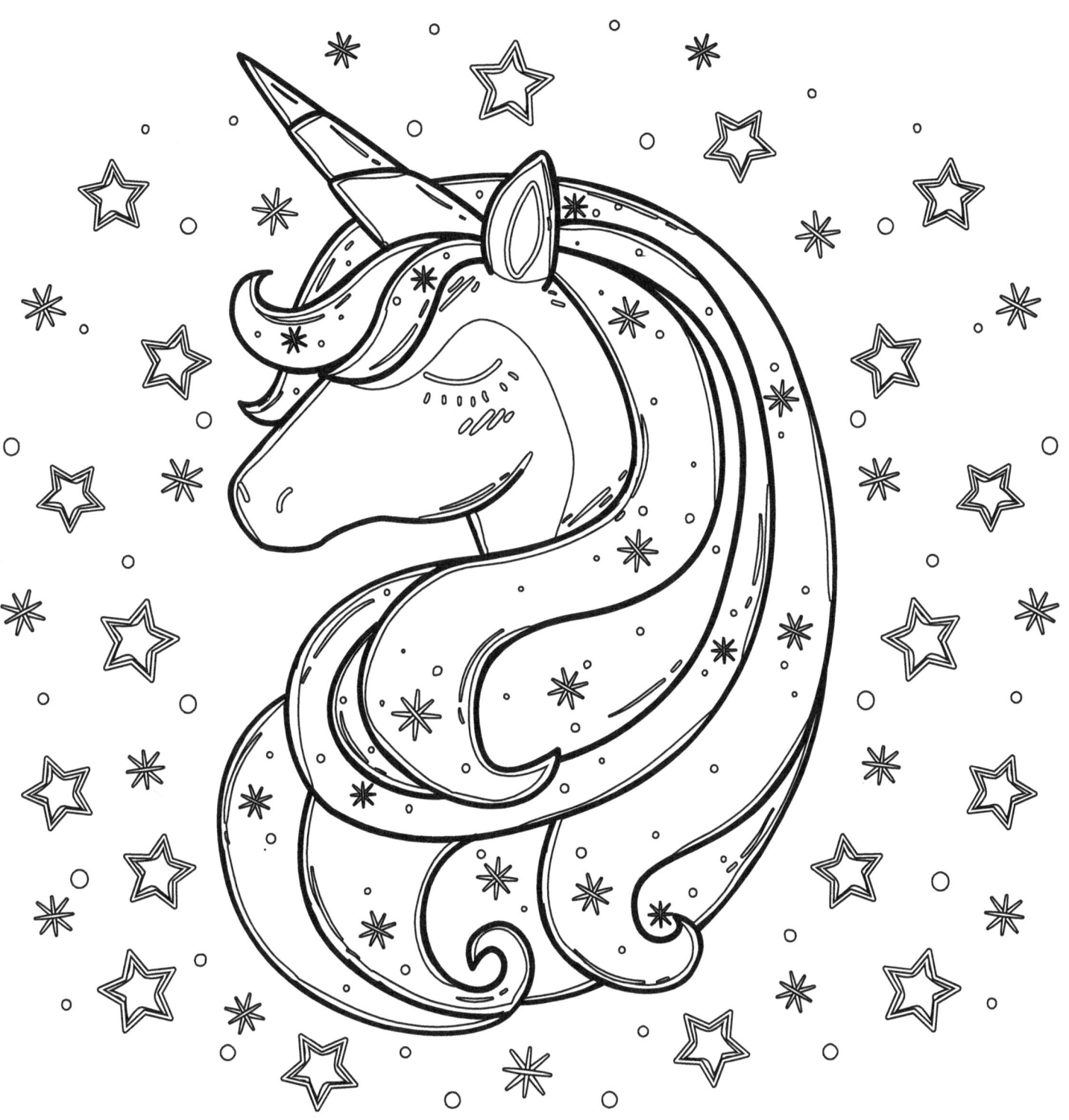

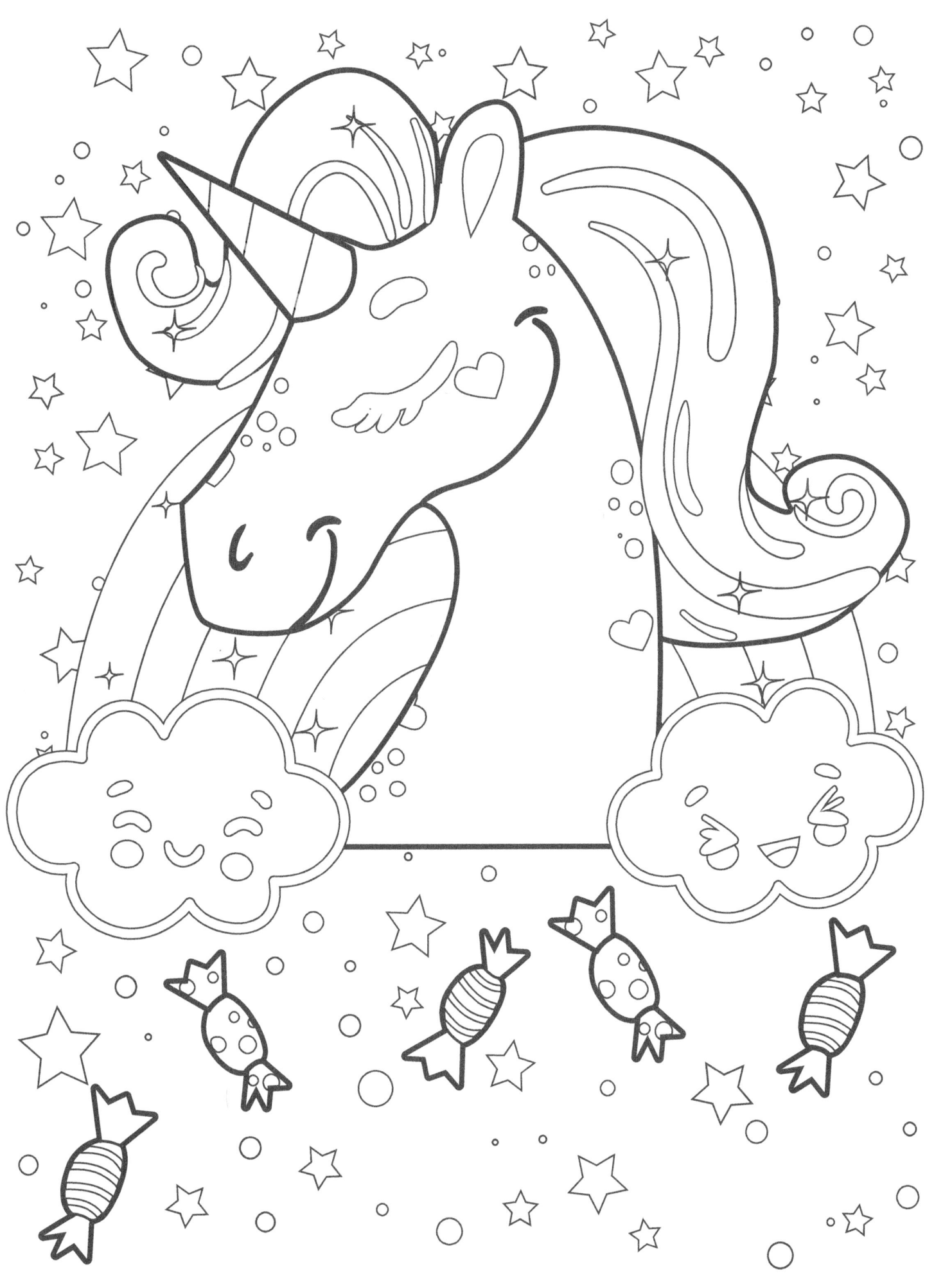

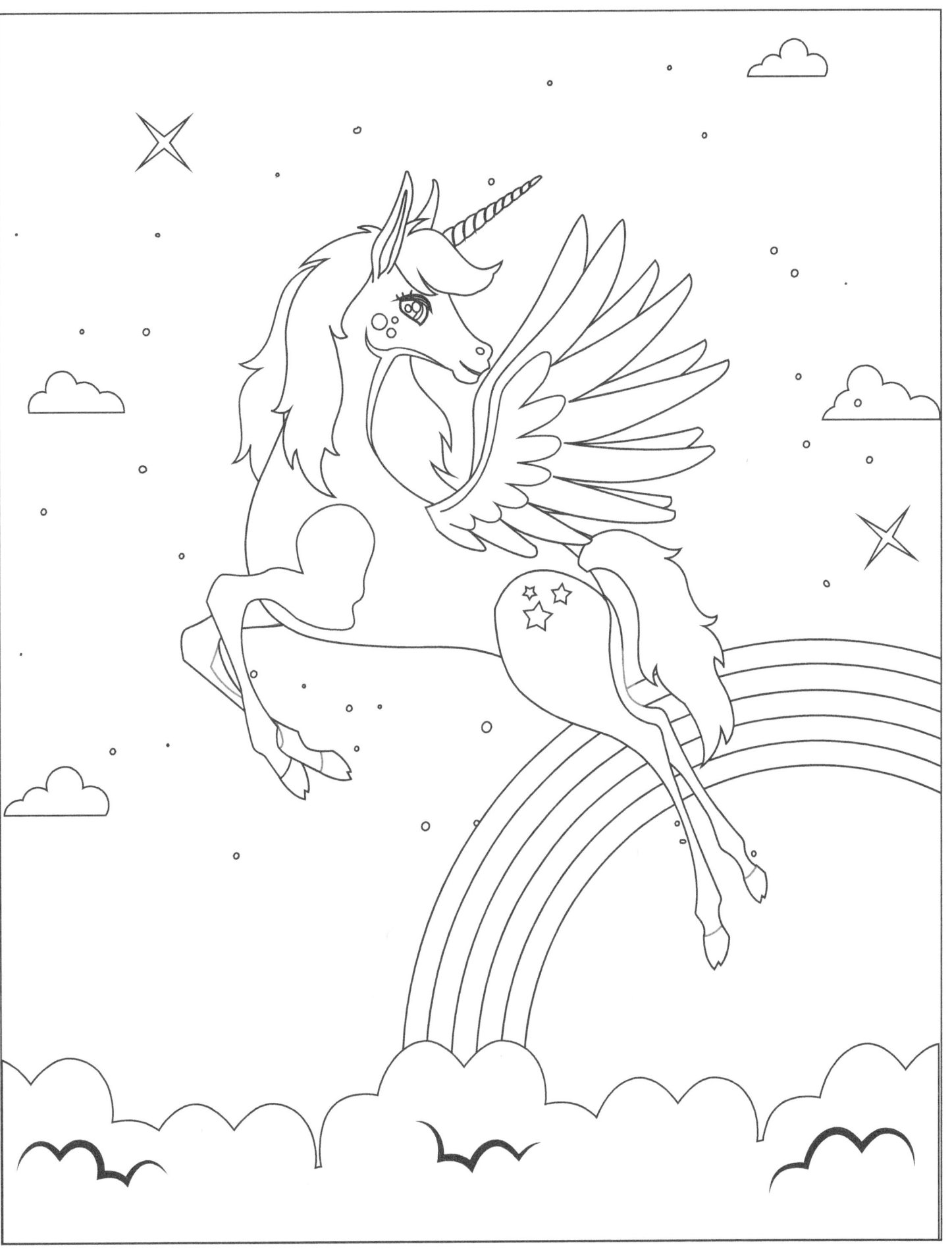

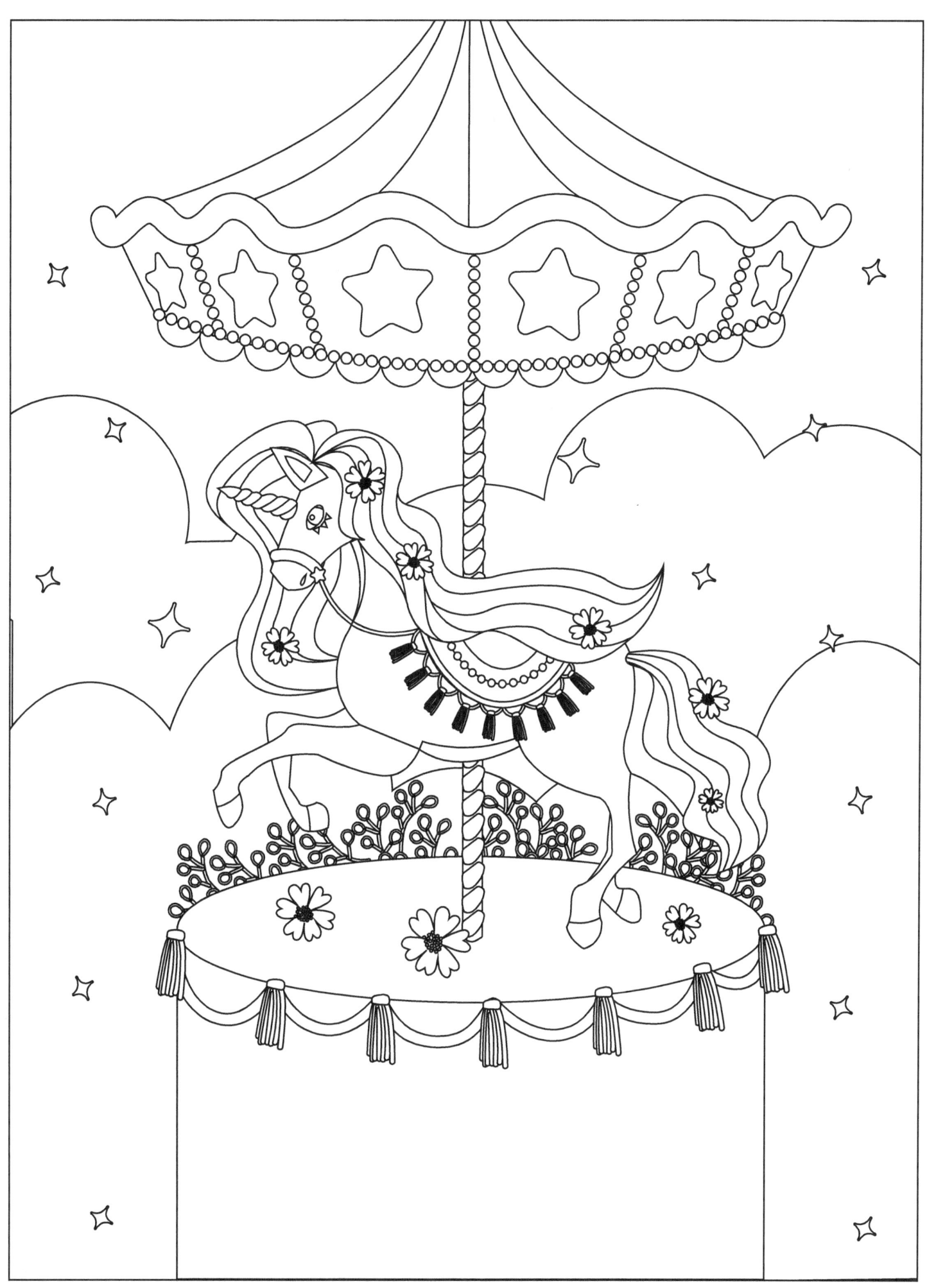

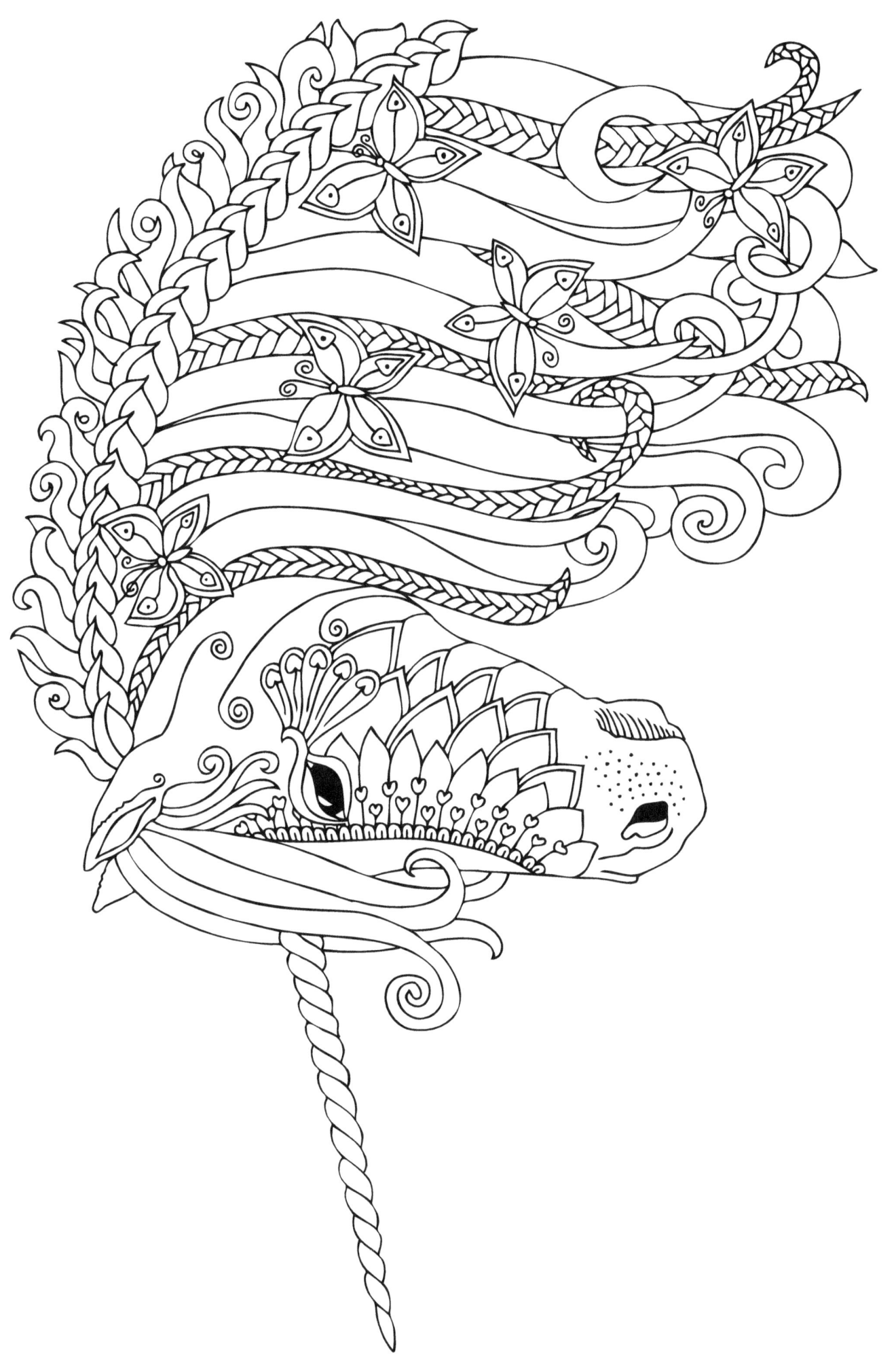

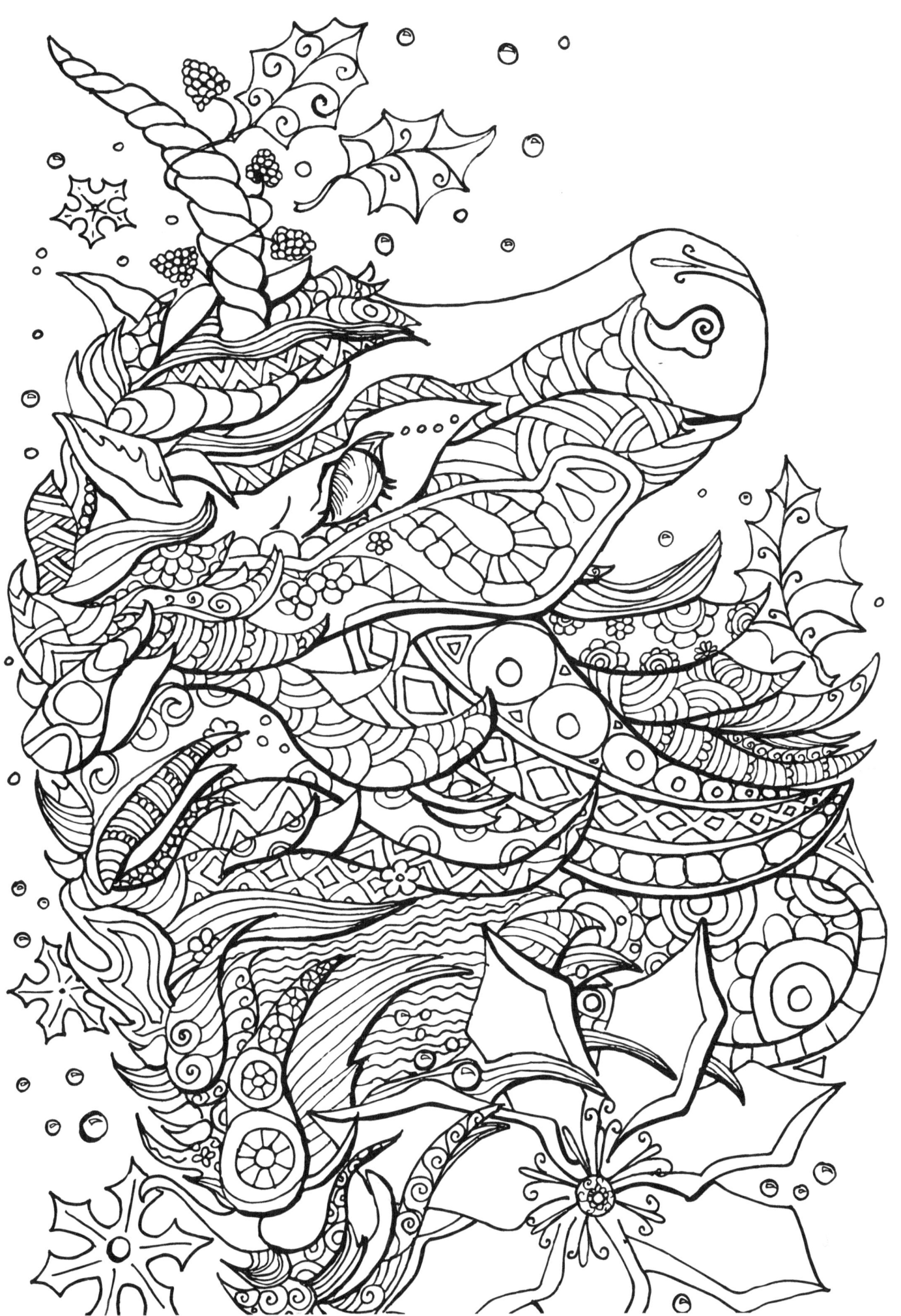

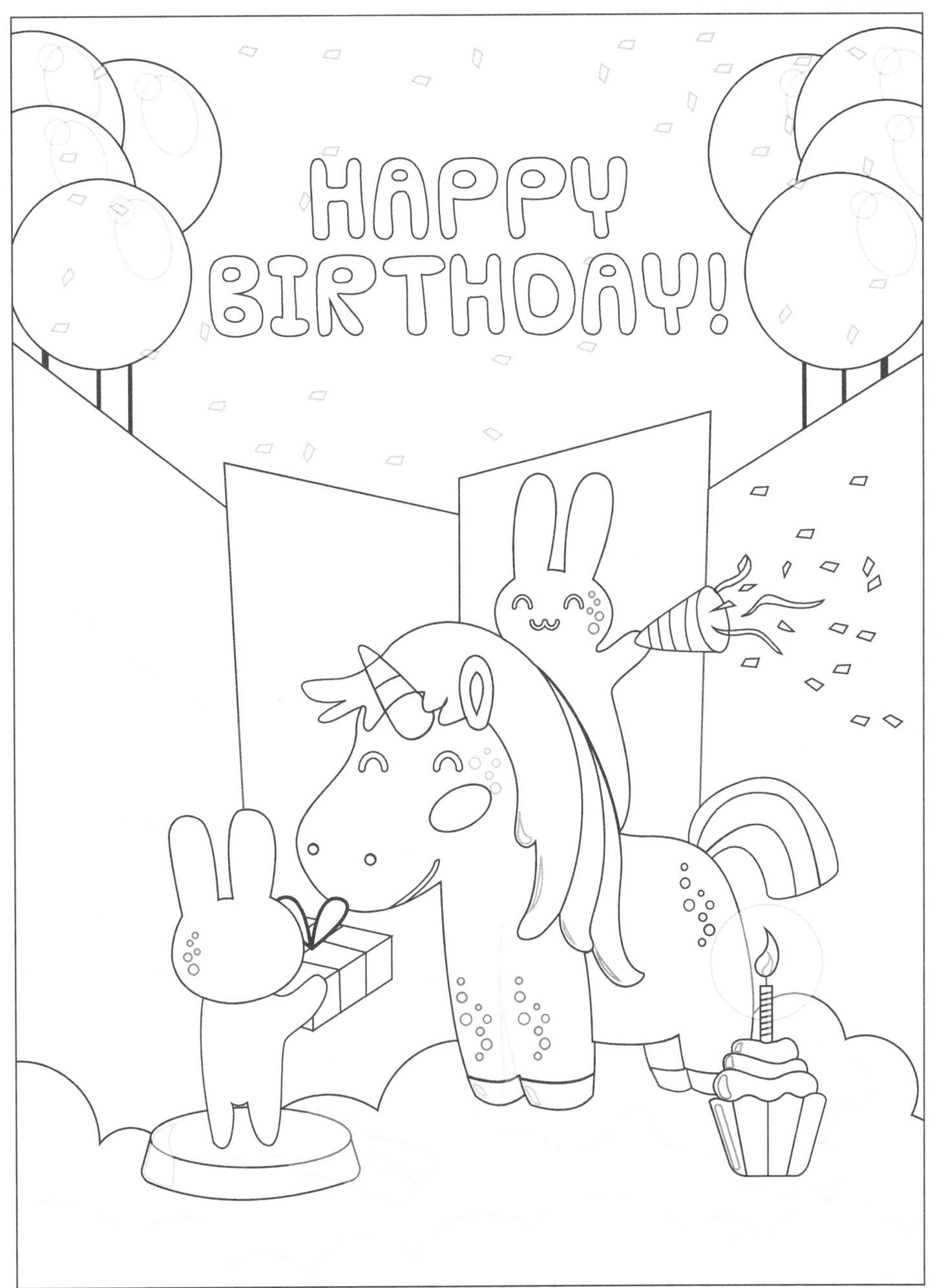

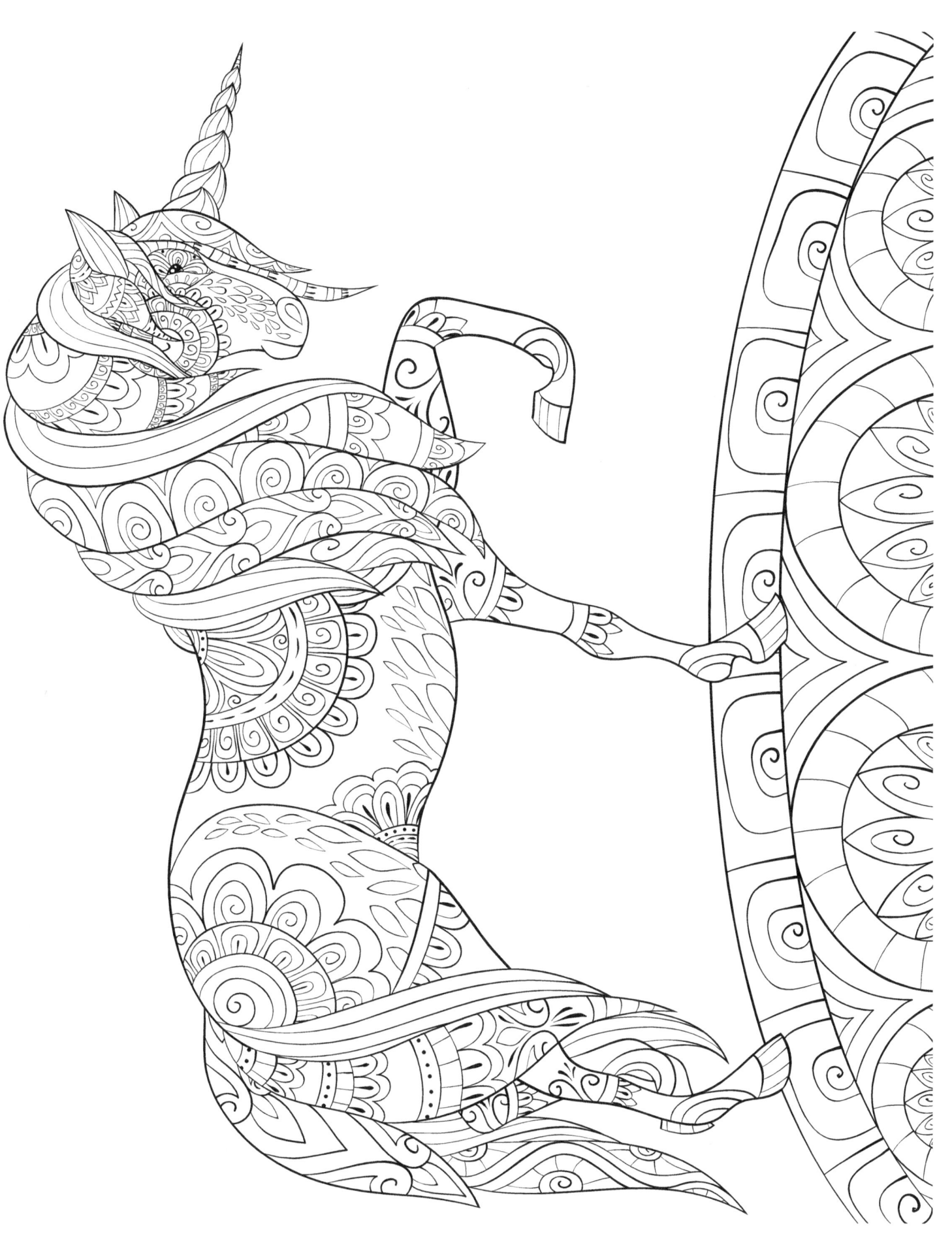

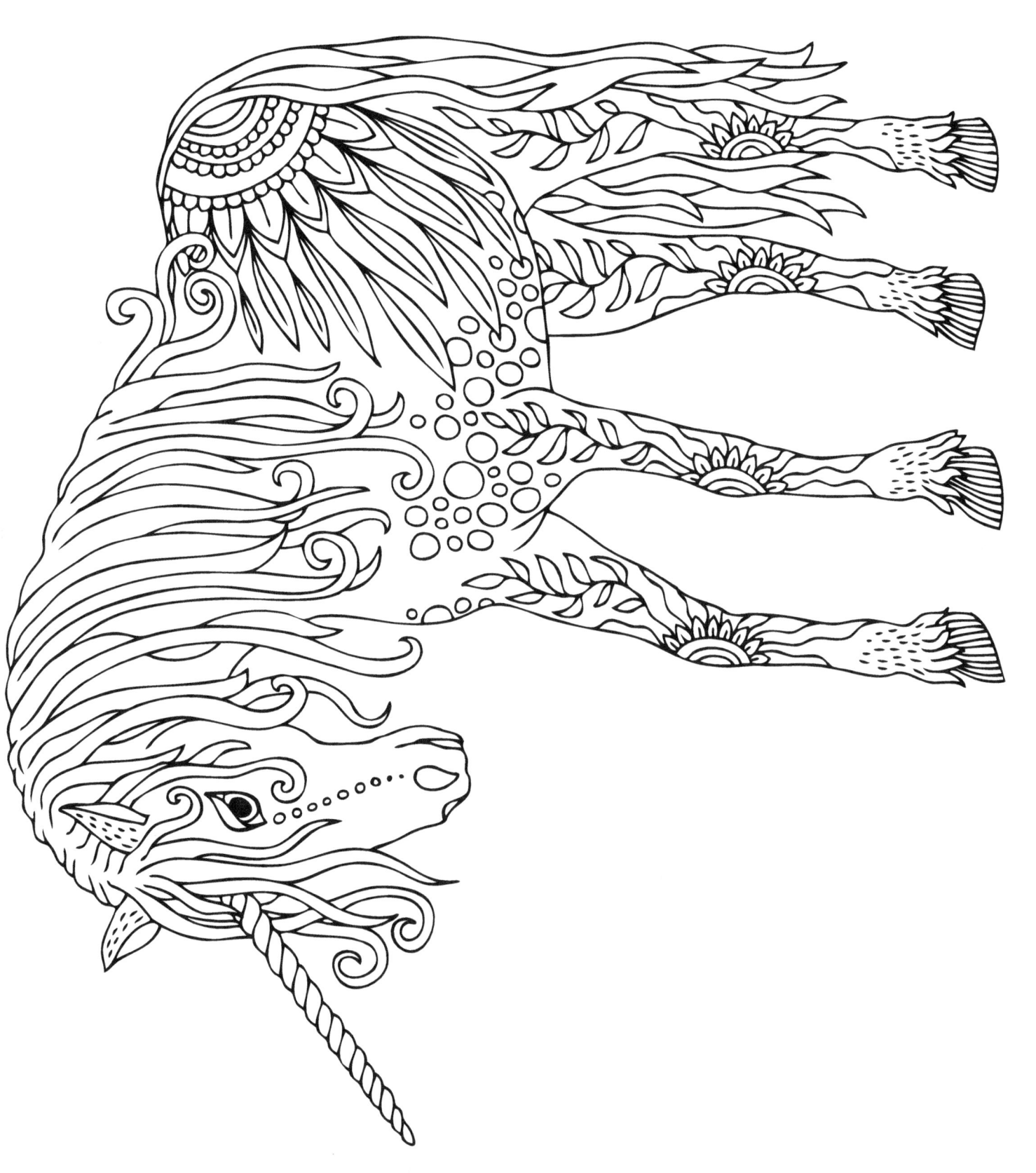

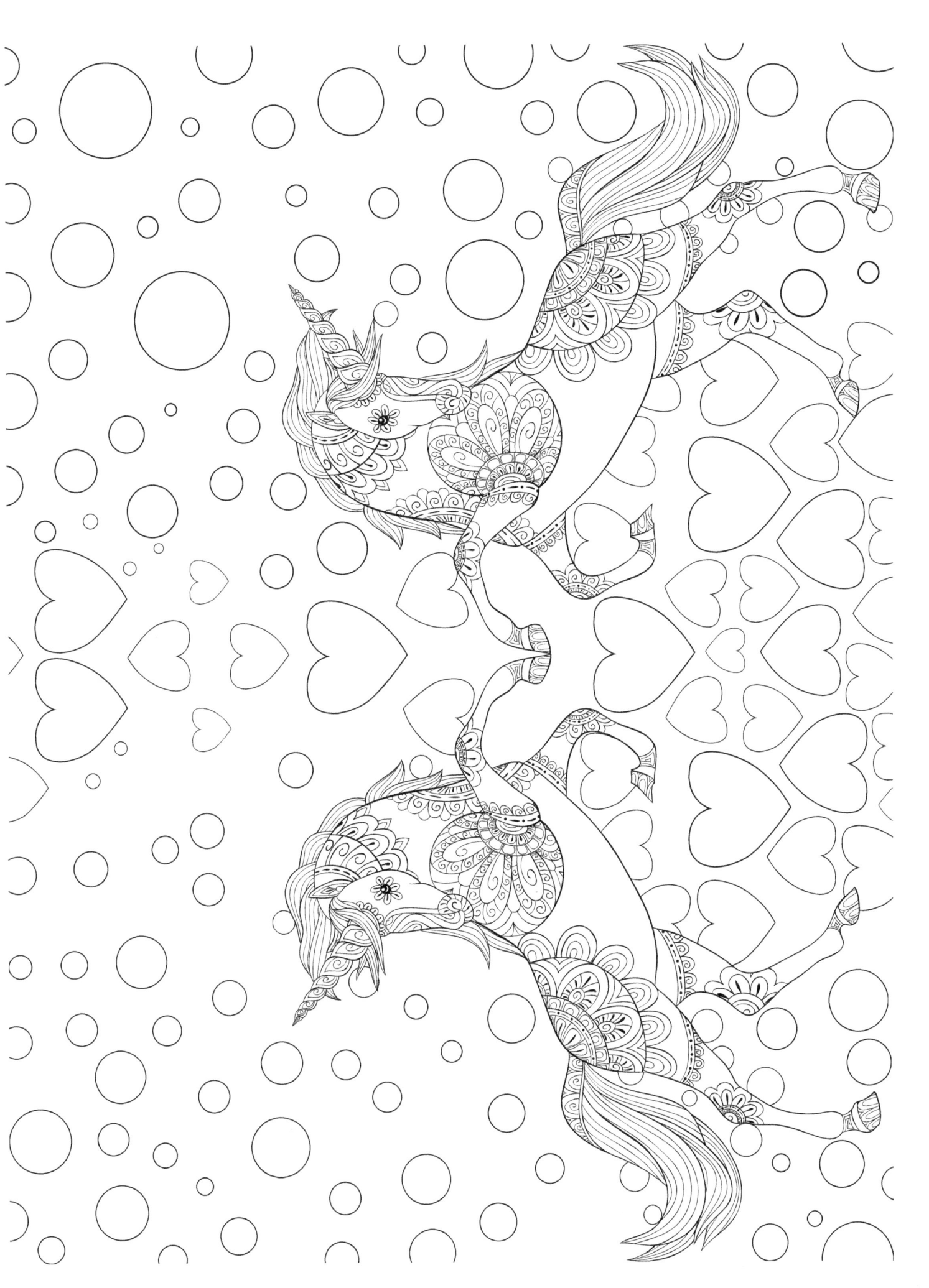